ADVANCE F

CW01082598

"While numerous guides focus on enhancing financial literacy, this book takes it a step further. It is dedicated to enriching your longevity literacy."

Prof. Tina Harrison, University of Edinburgh

"Dr Tom challenges the myth of financial independence and instead champions financial wellbeing – aligning money with purpose, stability and personal fulfilment. With a clear, science-based approach, this book offers a smart, practical guide to building wealth without speculation or fear-driven decisions. A must-read for anyone who wants their money to truly serve their life."

Karl Matthäus Schmidt, CEO of Quirin Privatbank

"This is a compelling and insightful guide to financial wellbeing in a longer life. Using a wonderful combination of engaging and relatable stories, historical context, behavioural science insights and thought-provoking questions, this book highlights how emotional intelligence and mindset matter as much as the numbers."

Emma Boardwell, Founder of Emotional Finance

"In Your Path to Prosperity, *Dr Tom offers a fresh and thought-provoking approach to financial wellbeing, moving beyond the traditional concept of financial independence. Instead of chasing wealth for its own sake, he encourages you to focus on a balance between financial security and a meaningful, fulfilling life.*

Drawing on behavioural science, psychology and real-life stories, Tom explores the challenges of living a 100-year life, where careers, relationships and financial needs evolve over time. He dives deep into the emotional and psychological aspects of money, showing how our mindset and decision-making impact our long-term happiness.

Rather than offering rigid formulas or quick-fix strategies, Your Path to Prosperity *provides a flexible and insightful guide to funding a happy, long life – one that prioritizes both financial wellbeing and personal fulfilment."*

Dan Haylett, Director at TFP Planning and
host of the Humans vs Retirement podcast

"In a world where longer lives are becoming the norm, this book is an essential guide to reimagining how we live and work. The traditional three-stage life of education, work and retirement no longer fits the reality of our non-linear journey, where we move in and out of different phases over time. It challenges us to think not just about financial security, but also about what brings fulfilment at every stage – through work, relationships, learning and self-discovery.

But it's not just individuals who need to rethink their approach – employers also have a crucial role to play. Recognizing the value of older workers and the benefits of multigenerational workplaces will be key to creating a future where people can contribute and thrive for longer, benefiting businesses, individuals and society as a whole. This book offers a compelling vision for how we can all embrace the opportunities of a longer life."

Mike Mansfield, CEO of ProAge

"Dr Tom has crafted a wonderful book that combines the practical financial strategies needed to fund a long and fulfilling life with insights from coaching psychology and behavioural science that will help you find fulfilment through discovering what truly matters to you. Living longer means rethinking how we plan our lives. The concept of retirement and our ability to fund it is changing rapidly. But living longer also means understanding our attitudes, beliefs, emotional reactions and self-awareness about what makes us happy and what we want long-term. After all, we will have a lot more time to enjoy it if we get it right."

Dennis Harhalakis, Founder of Cambridge Money Coaching

Published by
LID Publishing
An imprint of LID Business Media Ltd.
LABS House, 15–19 Bloomsbury Way,
London, WC1A 2TH, UK

info@lidpublishing.com
www.lidpublishing.com

A member of:

businesspublishersroundtable.com

Printed and bound in Great Britain by Halstan Ltd
ISBN: 978-1-917391-35-1
ISBN: 978-1-917391-36-8 (ebook)

Cover and page design: Caroline Li
Illustrations: Luisa Rachbauer

THOMAS MATHAR

YOUR
PATH TO
PROSPERITY

HOW TO FUND
A HAPPY AND LONG LIFE

LID

MADRID | MEXICO CITY | LONDON
BUENOS AIRES | BOGOTA | SHANGHAI

CONTENTS

FOR ROBBIE AND TILDA, OF COURSE

FOREWORD

My work at Orion Advisor Solutions is dedicated to helping advisors guide their clients to not just financial independence, but financial wellbeing. That's why this book by Dr Tom Mathar is something I've looked forward to reading ever since he approached me about the idea on a recent visit my son and I took to Edinburgh. The intersection of money and meaning has been on my mind recently, and Dr Tom walks readers through a range of important financial wellness concepts that both non-finance folks and seasoned practitioners can understand and act on.

Among the undertones in *Your Path to Prosperity* that struck a chord with me is the reality that the former work-life construct has been upended. Consider that, as the good doctor discussed with me recently on my podcast, the concept of managing 'money' has been around for tens of thousands of years. Money itself was broadly invented some 4,000 years ago. But it has only been in the last 150 years that we created the notion of retirement as it currently exists. Considering that, and having been told that my daughter, who turns eight this year, stands a 40% chance to live to 100, I see finances in a different light. The reality is that we no longer work until we die. That's great news, but it requires a better framework to maximize wellbeing throughout our (hopefully) long lives – both financially and internally. Dr Tom has created just such a framework in the book you hold in your hands.

Dr Tom lays out a new multistage life using the 50-30-20 rule – a simple yet powerful principle that emphasizes the importance of balance in financial planning. The rule homes in on allocating money for needs, wants, and savings.

The multi-stage-life also posits that retirement is no longer a clear endpoint, but one of a series of life transitions, and we know that humans are not a species so keen on change. As I think back on just my professional life, I've already had two very distinctive careers. I began my professional life as a clinical psychologist and now find myself having worked in finance for over a decade. Now, in my mid-40s, it seems probable I still have a few more careers in me. Even if you're reading this and in your 60s and beyond, Dr Tom describes and instructs how each life transition has the power to reshape you for the better. As I read, I found myself pausing at times to reflect on embracing ageing as a continuous adventure and not a mindless grind to get to the next money milestone.

What you are about to embark on asserts that all of us should keep a future-oriented mindset. I think of this like a pre-mortem – assessing all the things that could cause some plan to fail while pondering the fun stuff along the way. Dr Tom's forward-thinking approach will challenge you to discard conventional personal finance wisdom and reimagine your attitude toward wealth, what it means to be truly successful, and pursue a meaningful life.

If you're just starting out in your career, trying to build a nest egg or saving for another goal, you'll find helpful budget-centreed tips. This book goes a step further, though. As the financial stages of life become more blurred, Dr Tom offers a roadmap with action steps along the way. He'll even quiz you a bit. I believe the younger crowd also benefits from his teachings and stories that highlight that happiness and prosperity are not some far-off potential achievements, but available in the here and now. Even if you are older and feel you're behind on retirement savings, Dr Tom positions that hitting financial independence should be the primary motivator. It's his idea that financial wellbeing is available to everyone that I think you'll come to appreciate.

The scientist in me was drawn to how Dr Tom breaks the book into three parts. Part 1, drawing inspiration from Thomas Mann's *Buddenbrooks*, calls out the dangers of chasing wealth, as is commonly perceived. Part 2 connects money in ancient times to the complexities of modern finance. Part 3 guides readers through uncovering joy in the everyday form in a world inundated with distractions that pull us away from contentment.

At the heart of *Your Path to Prosperity* is this: your quest should not be about reaching retirement, but appreciating all the choices, challenges and opportunities that face you today as well as those that await you. As you're about to dive in, I encourage you to approach each chapter with an open mind and a willingness to challenge existing beliefs and assumptions about money's purpose. Dr Tom's rigour and thoughtfulness have improved my own financial journey, and I'm confident that you'll soon be able to say the same.

Dr Daniel Crosby
Atlanta, GA, USA
April 30, 2024

HOW WOULD YOU HAVE DECIDED?

If you were looking for an eye doctor, you'd have happily settled with someone like Dr Ingmar Zöller. His practice in central Berlin was a favourite among patients, with many glowing reviews online.

But Dr Zöller no longer takes appointments. The endless bureaucracy and monotony had drained his passion from a profession he once excelled in. So, in his mid-50s, he made a bold move: he hung up his white coat, closed his thriving practice and chased his childhood dream.

Dr Ingmar Zöller became one of Berlin's subway drivers.

A complete career shift, a plunge into a new life. Now, in a newspaper interview, he shares his greatest joy:[1] the early morning hours at Ostkreuz in Berlin. Here, he opens the doors of his train, watching as people hurry to work. In these moments, he feels part of something larger. The sight from his driver's cabin fills him with a profound sense of fulfilment.

Zöller's decision wasn't easy. He must have asked himself questions like these: *Should I stay on the safe and secure path of an eye doctor? Or follow my lifelong dream of working with trains? At 50-something, I could keep earning a solid income until retirement, and indulge in my train fascination as a hobby then. But what would I miss out on now?*

What would you have done in Ingmar's place? Would you have taken the same leap?

This book delves into the complex decisions we face today.

On the one hand, we all yearn for a life filled with purpose and joy. We seek experiences, activities and possessions that bring satisfaction and relaxation, as well as those that make us feel useful, skilled and valued. Discovering the perfect balance is no easy task.

On the other hand, we need and hope for stability and security – a safe home and the assurances that our loved ones are well cared for. Yet, we live in a world of rapid, constant change. Technological breakthroughs, economic shifts and global events impact our lives in unprecedented ways. This ever-changing landscape makes our decisions even harder. What seems secure today could be obsolete tomorrow.

This makes life and financial planning incredibly challenging.

Ultimately, we all face moments where we weigh our true desires against long-term security. *Is an unfulfilling job worth the stability it provides? Wouldn't life be better if … ?*

There are many reasons behind the widespread shortage of skilled workers. One major factor is that more people are realizing their current jobs don't meet their needs, interests, talents or expectations. Consequentially, they choose to retrain, start their own businesses or seek new employers.

These individuals take significant risks, leaving behind the familiar to start anew. Just like Ingmar Zöller.

Many people dream of starting over. But new beginnings aren't necessarily always a choice. Sometimes, change is forced upon them. Take Emily, for instance.

You might have met someone like Emily Hanley. She's in her early 30s, handing out samples of sparkling water in supermarkets.[2] It's not her dream job. She does it to pay the bills.

Until early 2023, Emily was a copywriter. She crafted advertising copy for websites, emails and brochures for various companies. She was doing well, getting a decent amount of work through her agency. But then everything changed. Her clients discovered artificial intelligence (AI). ChatGPT made Emily redundant – at just 30 years old.

Emily Hanley is far from an isolated case. You'd think that artists and creatives like her would be safe from robots and AI. Being a copywriter wasn't just fun for Emily; it seemed like a safe bet, too.

Now she had to reconsider: should she keep trying as a freelance copywriter? Should she stay in the creative industry? How could she adapt to this new reality?

What would you have done in Emily's shoes? Would you have handed out sparkling water in the meantime?

Balancing what we want with what gives us financial security is harder than ever. Technological change has always destroyed and created jobs. But the pace of change today is dizzying, thanks to the internet, mobile technology, AI and robotics. Never in history have we seen such rapid development and implementation of new technologies as in the past 30 years.

Emily Hanley's story shows how quickly life can change due to external factors like technological advancement.

But it's not just the job market that's forcing us to adapt. Personal and family events can also bring unexpected challenges and force profound decisions.

This is illustrated by the story of Martina Rosenberg.

At first, living above her parents' flat was a blessing for Martina and her young family. The grandparents were a great help, often stepping in to assist. But over time, this situation turned into the opposite: a stroke dramatically changed her father's life, and her mother was increasingly affected by dementia. The grandparents, once a tremendous help, became an enormous burden.

Martina faced a moral dilemma: should she place her parents in a care home despite promising she never would? How could she continue her career as a freelance lecturer while being there for her children and her parents? The psychological strain was immense. This conflict is poignantly captured in the provocative title of her book, *Mum, When Will You Finally Die?*[3]

What would you have done in Martina's place? Would you have moved your parents to a care home? Or worked less?

Ingmar, Emily and Martina all faced decisions typical of our time. You've likely encountered similar situations in which you had to weigh the pros and cons. For example:

- Should I choose a career that brings me joy or one that ensures a well-paying job in the future?

- Do I want to start a family? Can I afford it in the long term? What would I sacrifice? What would I miss out on?
- Should I work part-time and save on childcare costs, or work full-time for a higher income, even though much of it will go toward childcare costs?
- Should I stay in my unfulfilling job or invest in further education, even if it depletes my savings?
- Should I dine out frequently or take trips with my partner, or should we save for a stable retirement?
- Should I take risks and start my own business, or stay in a stable but less-fulfilling job?
- Should I stay in a burdensome relationship or risk a fresh start after a divorce?
- Should I retire early and possibly receive lower monthly pension payments or work a few more years to secure a higher pension?
- Should I sell my house and move to a smaller flat to reduce maintenance costs and benefit from the sale?

At the heart of all these considerations is the balance between present and future quality of life on one side. And present and future financial security on the other.

These are incredibly tough decisions, aren't they?

This book aims to help you find a path that meets your desire for pleasure and purpose in life, while also considering the financial aspects and enabling you to fund that life. That's true prosperity. It stretches beyond the financials to include purpose, contentment, relationships, health, and balance in all aspects of your life.

The concept of prosperity has long been a subject of reflection. James Allen's classic work with a very similar title, *The Path of Prosperity*,[4] delves into the idea of prosperity through the lens of personal virtue, self-discipline, and spiritual alignment. While Allen's approach focuses on inner transformation as the foundation of success, my approach in this book emphasizes not only the practical financial strategies needed to fund a long and fulfilling life, but also, using insights from coaching psychology and behavioural science, guidance on discovering what truly matters to you.

When James Allen wrote his book in 1907, we lived in a completely different time. Then, people focused on shorter life spans and simpler economic structures. Today, we live 100-year lives, filled with complexities, transitions and opportunities. What does that mean?

THE CHALLENGES AND OPPORTUNITIES OF A 100-YEAR LIFE

Today, many of our decisions are complicated by the fact that we – as a group – are living longer, healthier lives. This means that our choices impact not just today but possibly long into the future.

In 2016, psychologist Lynda Gratton and economist Andrew Scott talked about a "100-Year Life."[5] They highlighted that living longer means rethinking how we plan our lives. We need to be more proactive about how we shape and fund our extended lifespans to achieve personal fulfilment and long-term security.

They also pointed out that a 100-year life is a journey of multiple stages. Unlike the traditional three-stage life – education, work, retirement – a multistage life has more transitions, interludes and new beginnings. Just like Ingmar, Emily and Martina, who all started over, either by choice or necessity.

Many of us can relate. More people are reflecting on their lives, weighing their options and choosing new paths. Sometimes, they are forced to.

Fifty years ago, life was more straightforward: there were clear roles, life phases and responsibilities. Today, things are more fluid. So, where do we find guidance for making good financial and life-planning decisions? We can't rely on governments – they're much more likely to take a back seat these days. It's up to us – you and me, all of us.

That's exactly why I wrote this book – as a guide. My main message, which I'll explain in the following pages, is:

For happiness and prosperity in a 100-year life, we need money. This includes income, emergency savings, transition funds and other long-term savings.

This isn't surprising. But how much money should we earn? How much can we spend today? And, importantly, how much should we save – for emergencies, transitions and retirement? I will provide answers to all these questions.

But money alone isn't enough.

For a successful 100-year life, money is just one ingredient. Think of it like baking a nice loaf of bread: you need flour, water, yeast and a pinch of salt. You can't make bread with *just* flour, *just* water or *just* yeast. You need all the ingredients together. Similarly, for a successful 100-year life, money is crucial but is not the only factor.

So, what are the other ingredients?

The answer: just as with *money*, we need the right *money mindset*. This includes understanding our attitudes, beliefs, emotional reactions and self-awareness about what makes us happy and what we want long-term. We need emotional intelligence.

In this book, I treat these ingredients like a recipe, examining each one individually and how they fit together.

In Part 1, we'll focus on money and money mindset: the attitudes, beliefs and emotional reactions that shape our approach to money. Beliefs like "money doesn't grow on trees" or "these are my productive years" often influence our financial behaviour. Various instincts, such as the desire for instant gratification, also play a role. Understanding our thoughts and behaviours around money is essential for making better decisions and achieving better outcomes.

But there's much more to explore.

In Part 2, we explore why many decisions in a 100-year life are so challenging. We look at three things: first, why managing money is generally difficult for us. Second, why it's hard to rethink some of our cherished expectations about retirement – supposedly the final phase of the outdated three-stage model. Additionally, we examine some challenges related to ageing. In Western societies, ageing is often viewed as a process of loss. While this perspective is understandable, it's also limiting. We need to rethink it.

In Part 3, we focus on solving all these problems. The solution can be summed up in one word: self-knowledge! Self-knowledge or self-awareness is the key: if we understand what our beliefs and emotions drive us to do, which habits and instincts hinder (or help) us, and what makes us happy and fulfilled, then we can make better life decisions. And use money to enable that life. In this section, we'll look at various behavioural science studies that show what truly leads to a happy life. We'll also examine how to recognize harmful mechanisms in our daily lives: Black Friday, for example. Or the news.

To counteract our lack of thinking time – moments where we stop, slow down and reflect – each chapter includes a small mental exercise. These encourage you to think instead of act, to consider your own path to prosperity in a 100-year life. Some of these prompts will ask you to fill in blanks in the text. Others will allow you to evaluate or rank things. Yet others simply remind you why the challenges and opportunities of a 100-year life are so difficult to navigate and make the most of.

BEFORE WE START: FINANCIAL INDEPENDENCE VS. FINANCIAL WELLBEING

Before we dive in, I want to share one more story. Oliver's story. His story highlights why, in a 100-year life, we shouldn't just think about the future but also make decisions that benefit the present.

Who hasn't dreamt of not having to work anymore? To live life on their own terms, without financial constraints?

Oliver had this dream and pursued a plan to make it a reality. For a long time, he was a frugalist, sharing his savings tactics on his blog, "frugalisten.de." Readers learned how Oliver, a recently graduated software developer, resisted various temptations: no expensive holidays or new car. He continued living like a student, saving 70% of his salary to retire at 40.[6]

But then something unexpected happened. Something his savings plan didn't account for: Oliver became the father of a baby girl. This led to a change in course.

The future that once seemed so clear became blurry in the vibrant picture of the present. Saving for a future dream suddenly seemed less important. Why work and save for the future when he could enjoy his daughter's laughter and witness her first steps? Oliver reduced his working hours and, with that, his income and savings rate. Not only did he realize that the good life won't just be happening in the distant future, it's also happening here and now. And when choosing to spend more time with his family, he probably also sensed that it might pay off to invest in things other than his long-term saving plans. Invest in family time. Social connections. Oliver, too, will have weighed his options carefully.

What do you think? Did he make the right decision? Would you have done the same?

I certainly would. (In fact, I did! I took a few months of paternity leave in the first year after my twins were born.)

You've probably heard the saying, "At the end of life, no one wishes they had answered more emails." It emphasizes that there are more important things in life than emails. And that's true. But I also wonder: why should the thoughts of a person at the end of their life be wiser, more valuable, or more important than their thoughts at any point in their lives? Yes, of course, in retrospect, those emails won't have mattered at the end of life. But today, right now, they might be important. Or maybe not. It depends.

And Oliver would have thought along similar lines. What's important today? Not just in the future. And what's important beyond the money?

And I believe Oliver realized something else important. He wouldn't have put it this way, but I'll say it for him: financial independence is the wrong goal. Financial wellbeing is the goal.

The dream of financial independence is about living a life where money doesn't matter because you have enough of it. With financial independence, all the tough decisions we face in daily life become irrelevant.

- Quitting a job as a doctor to become a subway driver? No problem if you're financially independent.
- Losing your job to ChatGPT? No problem if you're financially independent.

- Caring for your parents and reducing work hours? No problem if you're financially independent.

The problem is, financial independence (at least for the longest part of our longer lives) is a fantasy.

There are many who try to convince us how easy it is to become financially independent and how obsolete the assumption is that you need to earn an income from work. Bitcoin, real estate, speed trading, you name it ... you'll find literally thousands of books, TED Talks and podcasts on the topic. I think if it was that easy, more people would be financially independent.

The fact is, money has to come from somewhere. And in a 100-year life, we need more money simply because we live longer. Generally, we have to work for our money. If or when we're finally living off our savings, we typically worked rather a long time to earn that money.

Financial independence is also a fantasy because it's based on the assumption that everything would be easier if money didn't matter. That's simply not the case. Theoretically, it could be so. Practically, it rarely is. Without the other ingredients for a successful 100-year life – the right money mindset, emotional intelligence, self-awareness – having more money doesn't make much difference. (I assume you are not living below the poverty line. In that case, more money really can have a big impact on overall wellbeing.)

We often overlook that acquiring large amounts of wealth usually comes with costs. Nonmonetary costs (for example, sleepless nights or strained relationships). Oliver realized this. Sure, if he had continued working full-time, saved 70% of his salary, and let those savings grow for a couple decades, he might have been financially independent in his mid-40s. But what price would he have paid? All the lost hours with his little daughter.

That's why it's about financial wellbeing, not financial independence. Financial wellbeing involves earning, spending and managing money in a way that allows us to live a good life today, tomorrow and in the future.

Simply put, the pursuit of financial independence too often comes at the expense of enjoying a fulfilling life in the present.

This idea isn't new. It has been echoed by philosophers, writers, economists, psychologists and others over the years.

Let's start there: with the insights of Thomas Mann, the literary titan of his era, from a century ago. While he didn't explicitly discuss financial independence or wellbeing, his work beautifully conveys the notion that prioritizing a balanced and meaningful life surpasses the singular focus on financial autonomy.

Are you ready?

Then let's begin.

Enter the Buddenbrooks.

PART 1

Money and Money Mindset: The Foundations of Prosperity

Here's a three-step guide to financial independence:

Step 1: Sell all your assets and possessions (your house, your car and that collection of vintage comic books you always thought would be worth millions one day).

Step 2: Buy a one-way ticket to Jarovnice in eastern Slovakia. Get yourself a cabin by the tranquil river.

Step 3: Live off your savings forever.

Now that you've moved to your budget paradise with all of your savings, it's time to stretch that money over the next 40, 50 or even 60 years. Budgeting? Unnecessary. Investing? Too complicated. Just live frugally and hope inflation doesn't eat up your savings too quickly. What could possibly go wrong?

Of course, this is a satirical guide.[7] It's meant to illustrate, once again, that financial independence isn't the right goal. Financial well-being – earning, spending and managing money in harmony with what makes you happy today, tomorrow and in the future – is the better goal.

"Financial independence" – it's a dream for many. The rat race they want to escape. The quieter workday without money worries. Or better yet: a life without work. All this could be yours if you were financially independent. So, people think, and they start to dream. Often mistakenly.

To illustrate this, let's go back to the 19th century. We'll look at a great story from northern Germany: the story of the Buddenbrooks. Don't worry, it won't be dry. No literature class. No highbrow intellectualism. Just real, relatable insights.

CHAPTER 1

LEARNING FROM THE BUDDENBROOKS' BIG MISTAKES

Why the Buddenbrooks? There are three good reasons.

First, the Buddenbrooks offer us a rare chance to look at whole life stories – from birth to death – in all their ups and downs. We don't just get snapshots or specific episodes of their lives. We get to experience their entire journey, from their first cries to their last breaths, along with all the decisions, challenges and turning points that shape a life.

Second, diving into another time and culture often acts as a mirror. This mirror helps us see our own beliefs and actions more clearly. It might be a past era, but many of the lessons in the novel have timeless relevance and meaning for us today.

Third, and this is really crucial: having substantial wealth does not guarantee a fulfilling and balanced life. The Buddenbrooks were undeniably wealthy, actively managing and expanding their family's business empire. But, despite their financial success, their lives were fraught with personal turmoil, strained relationships and a pervasive sense of unfulfillment. This underscores a fundamental truth: wealth alone does not ensure happiness or emotional wellbeing. Let's explore how the Buddenbrooks' relentless pursuit of financial success often came at the expense of their emotional and wider wellbeing, highlighting the importance of prioritizing financial wellbeing over mere financial accumulation.

The novel *Buddenbrooks – The Decline of a Family* was written by Thomas Mann and published in 1901. Thomas Mann was a literary rockstar of his time. He was behind some of the most famous novels of the 20th century. With the Buddenbrooks, he won one of the first Nobel Prizes for Literature.

The Buddenbrooks are a fictional merchant family from Lübeck (close to my hometown of Hamburg). They experienced their rise and fall over four generations. The book is mostly about the fall. It's a tough read. Although the story is fictional, it has autobiographical elements, inspired by Mann's own family. In the mid-19th century, when things were going downhill for the Buddenbrooks, Germany (like many other Western countries) was in a period of upheaval. Industrialization was kicking off, cities were growing rapidly. The Hanseatic city of Lübeck was a bustling trade centre on the Baltic Sea, dominated by merchants and craftsmen. For the average citizen, life was characterized by hard work, modest pleasures and hope for better times.

The Buddenbrooks, however, were part of the upper class and lived in luxury. They lived in a grand townhouse, where every room was filled with fine furniture, artwork and carpets. A house where the clatter of fine porcelain and the clinking of silverware were everyday sounds. In the mornings, they were woken by their servants, who served them breakfast. When they travelled, it was always in style. Whether it was summer retreats in the Alps or health trips to the Baltic Sea, the Buddenbrooks experienced things most of their contemporaries could only dream of. Evenings in the Buddenbrooks' house were exquisite! They hosted glamorous dinner parties attended by the city's elite. There was laughter, dancing and discussions until the early hours. The wine was, of course, only the finest!

Naturally, it wasn't all smooth sailing. The political turmoil of the time didn't leave them untouched. But overall, the Buddenbrooks had made it. They lived in wealth and privilege, far removed from the worries of ordinary citizens.

In short, the Buddenbrooks were the epitome of financial independence. While the vast majority of the population were day labourers, they lived off their successful grain trading business, income from real estate and other investments.

But what about their financial wellbeing? Well, that wasn't great at all. Let's have a look.

FINANCIALLY FREE, BUT PERSONALLY FAILED

Let's look at four members of the Buddenbrook family.

THOMAS BUDDENBROOK

Let's start with Thomas Buddenbrook, a name that commanded respect and high expectations in Lübeck. Even as a small boy with curly hair and sparkling eyes, Thomas had a knack for business. While other children played with marbles, he traded them for small profits: a budding businessman in the making.

As he grew up, responsibility came early (and he was very proud of it). He joined the family business, destined to carry on the Buddenbrook legacy. His business trips took him to the then-exotic Netherlands, where he not only secured lucrative contracts but also found his future wife.

When he was offered a seat in the senate, his ambition knew no bounds. *Senator Buddenbrook*, member of the Lübeck city council – it seemed like the perfect next step! Surely, this would impress his main rival, Hagenström. But was it truly his calling, or just a title he pursued out of vanity?

In his later years, he realized that life as a businessman wasn't always rosy. The competition was relentless, and Thomas struggled to keep up. There were bad investments here, poor decisions there. The grand new house he built began to look more like a monument to his hubris. It ultimately became a financial burden. Self-doubt plagued him: should he have gone to university after all? Would another life have been more fulfilling? The bright moments of his youth faded, and he was haunted by dark thoughts of a wasted life.

After what seemed like a routine dental operation, it was all over for him: half-dazed from the anaesthetic, the proud Thomas Buddenbrook collapsed, landing face-first (and with his buttoned-up white collar) into horse manure. There he lay, quite literally, in the shit. And so ended Thomas Buddenbrook, once the shining star of Lübeck – financially and personally ruined. Thomas Mann did not paint a flattering picture of his father, whom he depicted through the character of Thomas Buddenbrook.

What lessons does Thomas Buddenbrook hold for us today?

ADVICE FROM THOMAS BUDDENBROOK

Hello, I'm Thomas Buddenbrook. During my lifetime, I was an ambitious businessman in Lübeck, driven by high ambition and my family's expectations. Although I come from a bygone era, I hope you can learn valuable lessons from my experiences for your own life:

1. Be Brave and Open to Change
   If you feel that the path you are on doesn't align with what makes you happy, have the courage to make changes and explore new directions.

2. Vanity and the Pursuit of Status Are Fleeting
   Don't blindly chase recognition and social standing. Contentment often comes from the relationships and community we nurture, not from individual fame.

3. Evaluate Your Life as a Whole
   What seems important today might lose its significance tomorrow. Ask yourself if you might regret the path you've chosen at the end of your life.

Don't let the expectations of others or societal conventions restrict you, as they did me. Rather, attempt to live in harmony with your own ideas and values. Take the time to discover what success means to you personally, beyond the numbers. And how you can achieve it.

So, that was Thomas Buddenbrook. Financially free and independent. But his life was rather a failure.

CHRISTIAN BUDDENBROOK

Now let's turn to Thomas's brother, Christian. He was the black sheep of the family.

Even as a child, Christian had a talent that didn't quite fit with the rest of the business-minded Buddenbrooks. For example, he had the rather obscure talent to mimic people and situations so well that it made everybody laugh. His true passion and talents lay in theatre and the arts. While others dreamt of trade routes and profit margins, Christian got lost in the world of the stage and imagination.

His youth was filled with escapades and travels, adventures and a constant search for the meaning of life. But fate, or perhaps family tradition, pulled him back to Lübeck and into the family business. Here, he felt like a fish out of water. The business tasks didn't suit him, and he felt lost in the world of numbers and facts. So, his departure from the company was no surprise, even if the reasons he gave weren't entirely true. He talked about a desire for the independence that comes with self-employment and a dislike for big companies. But anyone who knew Christian knew these were just excuses. In truth, he yearned for freedom to pursue his real passion. However, in the Hanseatic merchant world, the supposed desire for self-employment was the only acceptable reason to leave the family business. His relationships, both familial and friendly, suffered from his decisions, often driven more by personal ambitions than communal considerations.

Of course, his own business was doomed from the start. Without business acumen and genuine passion for the trade, success was elusive. The failure was costly for his brother Thomas and the Buddenbrook family's wealth. And Christian led a sad, illness-ridden life, marked by disappointments, missed opportunities, and the knowledge of wasted time.

His relationship with his brother Thomas was strained. They were brothers, but they couldn't have been more different. While Thomas followed duty and tradition, Christian searched for a deeper meaning in life. But both paid a high price for their decisions. The rift between them shows how personal goals can deeply affect social bonds – and relationships.

From Christian, we can learn a crucial lesson: yes, we need to earn money. But, ideally, it's being earned in a way that brings personal pleasure and purpose. Christian's life path highlights the delicate balance between pursuing our true interests and meeting the demands of society and our financial environment. His story reminds us that, while it's idealistic to expect a perfect match between job and true self, it's also vital to seek a career that nourishes our interests and allows our professional persona to authentically reflect our core values. It's about finding that sweet spot where our work not only fills our bank accounts but also brings satisfaction. Importantly, even when forced to present our 'false self,' this self should still embody aspects of our true values and community ties, rather than merely reacting to external expectations.

**ADVICE FROM
CHRISTIAN BUDDENBROOK**

Hello, I'm Christian Buddenbrook. In life, I was the black sheep of the Buddenbrooks, the dreamer in a family of merchants. I come from another time, but I have a message for you.

1. Find Your Interests
   Don't spend your whole life trying to fit into a role that doesn't suit you. Discover your interests and talents and have the courage to follow that path.

2. Health Before Wealth
   Never neglect your mental and physical health in the pursuit of material success. In the end, it's your health that gives you the real freedom to enjoy life.

3. Live and Let Live
   My family had expectations of me. I couldn't meet them but they still supported me. Foster an environment where both individual freedom and communal support can thrive.

I wish I had learned these lessons earlier. Don't let others' expectations dictate your life. It's too short and too precious to spend it with regrets.

I accept that it might feel a little odd to receive life advice from fictional characters from the 19th century. But I do believe that sometimes it's these stories that open our eyes and show us what really matters in life. The Buddenbrooks may come from another time and culture. But their struggles, fears and dreams are universal. They reflect our own lives and decisions.

Maybe you're not a fan of literature or stories about long-dead wealthy snobs from northern Germany. But keep reading. It might be worth it.

TONY BUDDENBROOK

Now, let's focus on the sister of Christian and Thomas: poor Tony.

Tony Buddenbrook was the sunshine of the family. Her childhood was filled with cheerful moments and carefree days. She laughed often, played with her siblings and enjoyed the simple pleasures of life. But it soon became clear that her path in Hanseatic society was predetermined: a suitable marriage and motherhood.

A summer at the Baltic Sea resort of Travemünde was destined to change everything. There, Tony fell in love with a young man who wasn't of her social standing. It was a passionate (well, for the time) but forbidden love. Society, family and their expectations stood in their way. Tony knew she could never be with him, no matter how much her heart longed for him.

Instead, she married Grünlich, a businessman from Hamburg. On paper, everything seemed perfect: he was wealthy, reputable and promised security. But Tony felt nothing for him. Worse, she found him repulsive. Still, she complied and tried to see the positive side. For one, there were the bright lights of Hamburg. And being a member of the city's upper class also seemed appealing.

Alas, the marriage with Grünlich ended in disaster. He turned out to be a fortune hunter who only wanted the Buddenbrook family's money. Humiliated, she entered another unhappy marriage a few years later. And again, driven by the hope for a reputable, secure life, she married another businessman she couldn't stand. Things got worse. This marriage also ended in divorce, costing the Buddenbrook family dearly once more.

Tony spent the rest of her life in constant shame and embarrassment.

Today, equality and self-determination hold much more importance than in the mid-19th century. But today, also, I would argue, decisions often taken at a household level are likely to put women's long-term financial success at risk. How often do mothers, not fathers, work part-time to focus on child-rearing? How often do women still let their male partners handle finances for the future?

My research with heterosexual couples shows that women often decide on current expenses like groceries, clothing or Christmas presents – spending for the present. But when it comes to saving for the future or planning for retirement, men are more likely to take charge. (This is true even when women earn as much or more than their male partners.) This division of roles can lead to subtle yet profound economic dependence, leaving women in a vulnerable position, especially in the long term or in old age. Therefore, it's crucial for men and women to take the role of copilots not just in daily household budgeting but also in long-term financial strategies.

Tony Buddenbrook's story serves as a stark warning of what can happen when one denies themselves and leaves the long-term consequences of some high-stakes decisions to others. Her story warns us that involvement in all aspects of financial planning is essential for personal financial wellbeing. This means that everyone's got to educate themselves, stay informed and think through a decision's long-term consequences for each household member.

ADVICE FROM
TONY BUDDENBROOK

Hello, I'm Tony Buddenbrook. I had a happy childhood, was wealthy and financially independent. Yet, I made poor decisions and lived a life of shame and loneliness. I come from a different era, but I have a message for you.

1. Get Involved in Your Long-term Life and Financial Planning
    Educate yourself, stay informed and be involved in all financial decisions. If you're in a relationship, ensure that all parties actively participate in long-term life and financial planning.

2. Don't Forget What Gives You Personal Fulfilment
    In your life decisions, consider what brings you long-term satisfaction, rather than constantly meeting others' expectations or chasing material gains.

3. More Money Doesn't Automatically Mean More Happiness
    My marriages, primarily entered into for financial and reputation reasons, did not lead to lasting personal happiness or fulfilment. My experiences highlight the issues and limitations that arise when material wealth is prioritized over personal relationships and emotional wellbeing.

I wish I had learned these lessons earlier and I wish I had tried harder to shape my life on my own terms.

HANNO BUDDENBROOK

The last person we're going to look at is Hanno Buddenbrook.

Hanno Buddenbrook was Thomas's son, a sensitive soul in a world driven by hard business acumen. Even as a child, he showed a delicate nature, which manifested in his love for music, especially the piano. Every keystroke, every melody seemed to come from the depths of his soul.

Once, the family was sitting in the salon, and six-year-old Hanno Buddenbrook started to play. Tony Buddenbrook was ecstatic:

> "How the child can play! Oh, how he can play!" she cried, hurrying to him half-weeping and folding him in her arms. "Gerda, Tom, he will be a Meyerbeer, a Mozart, a—" As no third name of equal significance occurred to her, she confined herself to showering kisses on her nephew, who sat there, still quite exhausted, with an absent look in his eyes.

> "That's enough, Tony." the Senator [Thomas Buddenbrook] said softly. "Please don't put such ideas into the child's head."[8]

Naturally, Thomas Buddenbrook didn't want his son to become a musician. A musician? OMG! He was rather set on another path. The family business awaited, and Thomas was determined to prepare his son for it.

But Hanno and business? They went together like oil and water. Every attempt by Thomas to instil a business education in Hanno seemed to drive the boy further away from himself. This reflects Thomas Mann's own childhood, where he felt the pressure to meet his family's expectations rather than follow his own artistic inclinations.

Hanno's end was tragic. He died young from typhoid fever. During his illness, despite his youth, he showed no will to live. A young man whose vision of the future clashed so severely with his family's expectations that he lost all desire to live. If only he had the chance to connect with a future self shaped by his own talents, hopes and interests rather than his family's business expectations.

In our modern world, where individual self-fulfilment and pursuing personal passions are increasingly valued, Hanno's story and his tragic end should make us think. How often do parents, often with the best intentions, pressure their children to follow a certain path because they believe it's best for them? How often do they overlook what the children themselves say about what truly brings them pleasure and purpose?

We will explore this idea further in a later chapter: For our path to prosperity, it's crucial to establish a positive connection with our future self, a connection shaped by what genuinely matters to us, what drives us from within. For Hanno, this connection was destroyed. His future self was all about making money – ideally further growing wealth and assets. Perhaps the lack of positive, intrinsically motivated visions for his life contributed to his early demise.

Hanno's story is a stark reminder of how important it is to have an intrinsically motivated and positive connection to the needs of our future self. How can a negative vision of ourselves motivate us to care for our future? Why should we take care of our future self if it's someone we don't want to be?

ADVICE FROM
HANNO BUDDENBROOK

Hello, I'm Hanno Buddenbrook. I died very young, but during my life I felt a deep love for music in a world dominated by business and expectations. I want you to learn the following from my story.

1. Recognize the Power of Positive Visions
   Negative visions are counterproductive. No one likes working toward an anti-goal. Instead, seek to build a vivid and meaningful connection to your future self to help bridge the gap between who you are today and who you want to become.

2. Pay Attention to What Brings You Pleasure and Purpose in Daily Life
   Reflect on what your sources of joy and meaning are. Let this knowledge guide what you do day-in-day-out. And let this knowledge shape your future.

3. Stand Up if You're Being Pushed Down a Path That Isn't Yours
   If you see yourself elsewhere, say it. It might hurt in the short term but, in the long run, it's worth the temporary pain.

I wish I'd had the chance to find my own path.

SIGNPOST

This concludes our journey to 19th-century northern Germany.

Take to heart the lessons from the lives of the Buddenbrooks. A family that was financially independent in their time, with all the opportunities life could offer. Yet, they managed to tragically mess it all up. In the end, they failed not only financially but also personally.

- Thomas, the businessman who lost himself in responsibility and ended up questioning everything.
- Christian, whose talents and interests never aligned with a commercial life, ended in self-imposed exile.
- Tony, who handed over her long-term fate to the men of the family, opted for the status quo at critical moments.
- And Hanno, the delicate genius crushed between his father's expectations and his own passion.

You see, financial independence is not the ultimate goal.

Instead, financial wellbeing should be our true aim.

It's not just about having money. It's about earning, spending and managing money in a way that allows us to live happily today, tomorrow and in the future. If the Buddenbrooks had embraced this principle, Thomas might have found more time for himself and more peace. Christian could have pursued his artistic talents without financial pressure. Tony wouldn't have entered into unhappy relationships driven by economic status. And Hanno might have harmonized his music with his life, achieving both financial success and personal fulfilment.

Financial independence is often celebrated today as the ultimate achievement: a state where one is free from the need to work by accumulating a certain amount of wealth.

But this dream has a catch: what exactly marks the point of financial independence? Without a clear understanding of what we truly want – "Your money needs a 'why,'" as Daniel Crosby aptly puts[9] – it's easy to fall into a hedonic treadmill, continuously pursuing financial goals that never bring lasting satisfaction. Every achieved goal can simply fuel the desire for more, without delivering true contentment.

When we finally reach financial independence, without self-aware-ness about what gives our lives meaning and joy, it can become an empty triumph.

This is where financial wellbeing emerges as a superior goal. It transcends mere monetary success, encompassing overall wellbeing. Financial wellbeing seeks a balance between financial security and the pursuit of quality of life, personal talents, interests and meaningful goals. It adopts a holistic perspective: how can money contribute to a fulfilling and meaningful life?

The Buddenbrooks illustrate that wealth alone does not guarantee happiness or a balanced life. Their relentless pursuit of financial suc-cess often came at the expense of their emotional and social wellbeing. However, their stories offer valuable lessons and serve as a cautionary tale against financial independence itself. Instead, they highlight the importance of integrating wellbeing into our financial aspirations. By prioritizing financial wellbeing, we can ensure that our pursuit of wealth supports a rich and balanced life, rather than undermining it.

———————

Imagine yourself in the old town of Lübeck. You're here for the first time and immediately feel the historical charm. The narrow streets, the red brick buildings and the grand merchant houses speak of Lübeck's rich trading history. The legacy of a significant Hanseatic city is palpable everywhere.

You walk along Mengstraße to the Buddenbrook House, now a museum. This house, once the home of the Mann family, takes visitors into the life of a wealthy 19th-century merchant family and is part of Lübeck's cultural heritage.

Standing in front of the house, you're impressed by the imposing façade. The architecture, the carefully restored ornaments and fine details embody the pride and dignity of Hanseatic merchant culture. You can vividly imagine the lively hustle and bustle of the past. You also see the Buddenbrooks in your mind's eye: Thomas, serious and determined on his way to work; Christian, lively and unconventional coming from the theatre; Tony, marked by duty and regret; and young Hanno, sensitive and nonconforming.

In what ways are you like Thomas Buddenbrook?

Do you also have …

… an intense drive for financial success?

… a deep need for social recognition?

… a tendency to neglect your own interests, talents and abilities?

In what ways are you like Christian Buddenbrook?

Do you also have …

… a disinterest in business and financial matters?

… a tendency to lose yourself in fantasies or unrealistic dreams?

… difficulty committing to long-term goals or responsibilities?

In what ways are you like Tony Buddenbrook?

Do you also have …

… a lack of personal happiness which you sacrificed for financial security or status?

… deep regret over past decisions?

… a tendency to leave very important long-term financial matters to others?

In what ways are you like Hanno Buddenbrook?

Do you also have …

… interests and talents in pursuits that aren't obviously marketable?

… little interest in material or financial matters?

… a negative connection to the desires and concerns of your future self?

If you find some 'Buddenbrook' in you, turn back a few pages and heed the advice of your alter egos.

The Buddenbrooks didn't live a 100-year life. When Senator Buddenbrook (or rather, Thomas Mann's father) died at only 49, he left behind
not just a declining family business, but also a poignant reminder of
how wealth and legacy, pursued without reflection, can lead to emptiness and misery.

In our era of the 100-year life, it's understandable that we strive
for financial independence. The pressures of navigating technological change, finding a fulfilling career, worrying about retirement and
meeting family obligations are overwhelming. In this context, the
allure of financial independence – escaping these stresses through
careful planning or clever investments – is undeniable. It offers a
seemingly straightforward promise: solve your financial problems,
and you'll solve your life problems.

But this goal is based on flawed assumptions. First, it assumes that
the alternative to financial independence is financial dependence.
Of course, no one wants to rely on others for survival. But between
these two extremes lies a more dynamic reality: a life where financial
interdependence – working, saving, sharing resources and adapting – is
necessary to navigate the complexities of multistage lives.

Second, financial independence presumes a three-stage life model
of education, work and retirement. It appeals because it suggests that,
with enough effort, we can bring the third stage – retirement – closer.
However, in today's multistage lives, education isn't confined to youth,
work isn't a linear path and retirement often involves multiple transitions rather than a clear-cut final stage. In this context, the financial
independence ideal isn't just outdated but naive: the notion that one
can ever be completely free of financial concerns oversimplifies the
realities of living longer, more complex lives.

The Buddenbrooks teach us another vital lesson. Their pursuit of
wealth and status blinded them to more important questions: what
makes life meaningful and enjoyable? How do we balance ambition
with health, relationships and personal fulfilment? Ironically, their
fixation on financial success led to decline. Their story reminds us
that money alone cannot create a life of happiness or purpose.

Rather than chasing the elusive and unrealistic goal of financial
independence, the focus shifts to true prosperity. This means using

financial resources not as an end in themselves, but as a means to supporting a life rich in purpose, connection and balance. True prosperity is about making financial choices that align with core principles, enhance present happiness, and prepare for the transitions and uncertainties of the future. It acknowledges that life's worth isn't measured by the size of a bank account or the age at which work can be abandoned, but by the ability to fund a happy and meaningful long life.

In embracing the concept of true prosperity, life's complexities are not something to escape but to engage with thoughtfully, ensuring that money serves life – not the other way around. This perspective offers a more sustainable and fulfilling way to navigate the richness of a 100-year life.

CHAPTER 2

FINANCIAL WELLBEING - FOR A LONG AND HAPPY LIFE

Financial wellbeing rests on two pillars: 'money' and 'money mindset.'
Let's start with the first one: *show me the money*.

YOU CAN'T DO WITHOUT MONEY

Two friends of mine from university have become filmmakers. One of them, Anna, follows her passions and her heart. She makes documentaries in remote places where creative solutions to major human problems are found. Her films reflect her love for detail and her dedication to authentic storytelling.

Anna consciously chose to stay away from mainstream filmmaking. She doesn't want sponsors and commercial interests to limit her creative freedom. She doesn't want to make any compromises to make her films appealing to the masses. Instead, she operates on the fringes, presenting her work at small film festivals.

Financially, Anna faces challenges, as she often relies on government grants. She lives modestly in a suburb of Berlin.

My other friend, Simona, took a different path in the film industry. She works as a film producer in London, involved in larger commercial film projects. She enjoys being involved in films that tell stories that touch her audience and give them a good time.

Simona understands and shares Anna's concerns about sponsor influence. She also gets frustrated by the compromises she has to make with distribution channels. But she believes that, through larger productions, she can reach and positively impact many viewers. She sees sponsors and marketing strategy compromises more as part of a game she has to play. She's more pragmatic than Anna.

Simona is financially very stable. She saves money for her financial security. Although she respects Anna's artistic integrity, she also sees that the budget for independent filmmakers is often limited. She believes that, sometimes, you need to make compromises to achieve your dreams and ensure your financial security.

I think Simona is right: it's definitely worth following the Buddenbrooks' advice to know our interests, talents and needs and earn, spend and manage money in harmony with them. On the other hand, we also have to play the bigger game because we need money, income and savings; we need to handle debts smartly, and put money aside for transitions and later life. With longer lifespans, the need for financial resources increases. You can live modestly, maybe on £20,000 a year. But if you live 25 years longer, it means you need an additional £500,000 for your cash flow.

It's a simple calculation: £20,000 times 25 years = £500,000. But it also shows why financial wellbeing in a 100-year life is so challenging. You can't do without money.

WHY A STABLE INCOME IS IMPORTANT

Various examples highlight the importance of an income in our lives. When we think about the negative psychological and emotional effects of unemployment, it becomes clear how vital economic stability is for our overall wellbeing. People struggling with unemployment face not only the immediate stress factors of financial insecurity but also a spiral of difficulties like weakened self-esteem, increased anxiety and higher susceptibility to health problems. A steady income acts like a protective barrier against these challenges and underscores its fundamental importance.

But stable incomes don't just prevent misery. They allow participation in the good things in life. The British Pensions and Lifetime Savings Association[10] illustrates this in a report on Retirement Living Standards. Various retirees from different backgrounds and all parts of the country talk about what they need money for in daily life.

One retiree describes how important it is to be able to pay for a Netflix subscription. He says something like, "My partner's quality of life wouldn't be the same without Netflix … these things used to be luxuries, but in certain circumstances, they become necessities, don't they?"[11] Another retiree talks about how important it is to be able to afford eating out, as a restaurant visit, once a luxury, is now part of what it means to live in a modern society.[12] These statements highlight that an income not only covers basic needs but also enables participation in activities that are considered part of modern life, like entertainment and social interactions. They show that financial means protect not only against poverty but also provide access to quality of life and social inclusion.

It's a simple point but one we often forget. Without money, life quickly becomes miserable and incredibly tough. I personally know many people who say, "Money isn't *that* important" or "There are more important things than money," and therefore make everyday life decisions for themselves and their families that I fear they might later regret.

That doesn't mean we should always strive for more money. Money makes life easier when you don't have much of it. But the extent to which it makes life easier doesn't grow with income or wealth. The Buddenbrooks are a good example of this. Once you've reached a certain level of wealth, other things become more important.

The insight from various behavioural science studies is that the point at which more income contributes to more wellbeing might be lower than expected.[13] Therefore, it's about earning an income that is 'good enough.'

Literary critic Marcel Reich-Ranicki put it nicely when he said, "Money alone doesn't make you happy. But it's better to cry in a taxi than on a tram."[14]

WHY PLANNING IS IMPORTANT

Marie Ellis runs the "Broke Girl in the City" blog. Its mission is to help people live their best lives regardless of their budget. It's a blog that considers many of the hard lessons Marie Ellis has learned herself.

When she started university, Marie Ellis was already in debt; but then it was perhaps considered a way of life. She recalls how money was never her strong suit. Fortunately, though, at least for a while, she was resourceful. At university, she mostly worked behind a bar, but she also always took on other jobs to make ends meet.

When moving to London, her debt spiralled. In one of the most expensive cities on the planet, her first £5,000 loan was followed by credit cards, personal loans, refinance loans and the worst of them all: payday loans.

Over the years, she amassed a staggering £35,000 of personal debt. Her credit rating plummeted and, by 2011, she was relying on payday loans, using half of her salary just to service her debt.

Despite maintaining a detailed budget planner that accounted for every penny, she was broke from payday to payday, never having enough money to get through the month.

Marie rarely bought clothes or went on holiday. But she loved going out. That's perfectly understandable: London is one of the most expensive cities in the world, but it's also one of the most vibrant and culturally rich places, offering endless opportunities for socializing and entertainment. Working in very sociable industries, constantly making friends who were in the know about unique experiences, meant she was always out somewhere, enjoying that vibrant London nightlife.

But that lifestyle also got her into big trouble.

Debt is, in many ways, a double-edged sword. On the one hand, it can serve as an important driver for change and opportunities. Few people have the immediate financial means to buy a house outright. And through debt in the form of mortgages, the dream of homeownership becomes attainable for many. Debt can also be a tool for ambitious entrepreneurs to secure financing. Students worldwide often rely on student loans. These loans are investments in their futures. They enable them to pursue higher education and have the prospect of improved career opportunities. All these are examples of good debt: when used to buy something that costs less than it earns.

The other edge of this sword is sharp, though. And if you're not careful, it can leave deep wounds. When debt is used to buy things that lose value over time (or immediately – like Marie's nights out), it can become a heavy chain. It can tie people to past decisions and prevent them from moving forward. Examples of this include credit card debt from impulsive purchases or personal loans with relatively high interest rates. These are examples of bad debt, which can quickly spiral out of control and lead people into financial disaster.

Many studies, including research at Aegon's Centre for Behavioural Research, show how precarious the debt situation is for many: too many people owe too much. A high proportion would say of themselves, "I have too much debt compared to what I earn."

So be cautious with debt. It can quickly make life miserable. When taking on debt, assess whether it's good or bad debt. Debt is good when it has a realistic chance of generating long-term value or income. It's bad when it's taken out for consumer goods or services that don't create lasting value. Make sure your monthly debt payments – including mortgages, credit cards, car loans and student loans – don't exceed one-third of your monthly gross income before taxes.

When planning your finances, it's also important to consider potential interest rate increases. While low-interest periods offer more favourable credit terms, unexpected rate hikes can increase your monthly repayments and strain your budget. It's wise to consider long-term interest rates and plan for a financial buffer to protect against such fluctuations. Consider using fixed-rate loans where possible to secure predictable monthly payments and minimize the risk of interest rate increases.

WHY LIQUIDITY IS IMPORTANT

"Life is like a box of chocolates," says Forrest Gump in the eponymous film. "You never know what you're gonna get." Indeed, we don't. While some events bring joy and happiness, others can shock us and throw us off balance. I often speak about unexpected events happening and was still surprised when last year, within a short period of time, our washing machine died, water leaked through the roof and the kitchen drain got blocked. It hammered it home: it really does happen. And the point is, of course, such events can quickly result in financial stress. And that's often the last thing we want to deal with on top of the issues at hand.

This is where liquidity comes into play. The term 'liquid' refers to assets or funds that can quickly be converted into cash without losing value. Investments in stocks or real estate may require time to liquidate or be subject to market fluctuations. But liquid assets are immediately accessible. These funds are typically held in easily accessible ways such as checking or savings accounts.

I suggest holding liquid assets in two types of reserves. One is the rather well-known 'emergency fund.' The other is a perhaps less well-known 'transition fund.'

The Emergency Fund

Financial experts usually advise that a person should save approximately three months' worth of salary as an emergency fund. Perhaps a little more if you're self-employed. The logic is simple: if the car breaks down, the fridge gives up or the shower leaks into the neighbour's apartment, this fund provides a financial buffer. It allows you to handle these unexpected expenses without resorting to high-interest debt or disrupting your regular financial obligations and established lifestyle.

Three months' salary might seem high, maybe even unattainable. However, achieving this goal is not as distant as it might appear. A simple commitment – where you note down to yourself that you commit to saving a certain amount by a certain point in time – can work wonders. This is shown by the results of the study by Nava Ashraf and others:[15] in the most financially constrained communities in the Philippines, savings rates skyrocketed when people entered into a simple commitment contract. It shows that, with a bit of determination and strategic planning, even seemingly unreachable goals can become a reality.

The Transition Fund

We have already touched on the concept of a multistage life and the new way of looking at our life paths. We no longer live the conventional three phases of education, work and retirement. Many of us now experience numerous transitions, such as retraining, career changes or a return to education at various stages of life. This path, while filled with opportunities, also brings its challenges. To navigate these transitions, a financial means called the 'transition fund' is essential.

This fund is not the same as an emergency fund. The emergency fund is a safety net for unforeseen crises. The transition fund is specifically set aside to provide financial support during one of our transitions. Think of the stories at the beginning of this book, of Dr Zöller, Emily, Christina and Oliver. Each of them, at different stages of life, faced significant turning points. In these times, a transition fund is not just a protective barrier; it is also a facilitator of change.

Determining the exact amount for a transition fund might seem tricky. Needs vary, and life's course is often unpredictable. A general guideline, however, might be to save about six months' worth of net income. This provides a solid basis to take sabbaticals, pursue education, overcome periods of unemployment following redundancy or meet family needs without the looming shadow of financial strain.

Where should this money be placed?

Since the money is not needed often and might only be accessed every five to ten years, I personally avoid keeping it solely in a Cash ISA, savings or bank account (the first is where I'm keeping money from the emergency fund). Instead, I have invested it in a balanced investment strategy, combining various types of assets through a very low-cost fund to promote growth and reduce risk over time.[16]

This approach means that the value of my transition fund is likely to grow faster than inflation while remaining relatively stable in case I need to access it during tough times. The key is to ensure these funds are accessible relatively quickly to finance transitions when needed. Therefore, they should not be tied up in instruments with long payout periods, even though they are invested. In the UK, Stocks and Shares ISAs are a great vehicle to hold transition funds.

You might never need to tap into your transition fund savings. If life, including its transitions, goes smoothly, the savings held here can be integrated into your retirement plan. Therefore, building this fund is a step without regret. The savings in the transition fund are there if you need them. And if you never need to finance transitions, the savings will be useful later on.

Retirement Pots

Now we come to a crucial point: saving for retirement.

For most, retirement is one of the few certainties in life. Or rather, the likelihood of retiring is quite high. The timing – when you choose or can afford to retire – may differ from the original assumptions. Moreover, the expected quality of life during those years post-work is unpredictable. Most envision retirement as a peaceful period, free from daily toil. But without solid financial foundations, the dream can quickly turn into a struggle. Limited resources lead to a retirement with financial constraints and unfulfilled expectations. I've often heard retirees say something like: "I saved £100,000 and thought it was a huge sum. Why did no one ever tell me it wouldn't be enough? Far from enough?"

In the ups and downs of a multistage life, retirement might not necessarily happen overnight. It might be something we gradually ease into. But some circumstances might force people to slowly ease back out of it. In many Western countries, there's a growing gap between state pensions and the actual cost of living. The limitations of public pension systems become painfully evident as retirement approaches.

A common rule of thumb is that we should aim for an income in retirement of about 70–80% of our last salary. For instance, if you earned £30,000 in the year before retirement, then you might aim for a retirement income of £21,000–24,000. However, some argue that a target of two-thirds of your final salary may be more than enough, especially if you own your home and have lower expenses as you age.

Retirement researcher David Blanchett has identified a pattern that he jokingly calls "the retirement spending smile."[17] It gets its name because, in the early phase of retirement, spending tends to be high (often on things like travel). In the middle phase, as people settle into new routines, spending usually drops. Toward the end, however, costs begin to rise again, often due to healthcare or long-term care needs. This pattern forms the 'smile curve.'

Both perspectives suggest that the conventional rule of thumb might not suit everyone, as it doesn't consider the multiple retirement realities people live nowadays.

In either case though: the state pension is unlikely to suffice. And to bridge the income gap left by state pensions, many rely on the power of stock markets, using products like SIPPs or employer pensions in the UK; or IRAs or 401(k)s in the US, which are designed to maximize pension benefits.

COMPOUND INTEREST – A SIMPLE GUIDE

Compound interest means that interest starts earning its own interest. Over time, this leads to significant growth in your savings.

You can think of compound interest like planting a tree: when you initially plant a seed (your initial investment), it starts to grow. As it grows, new branches develop (this is your interest). Over time, these branches start forming their own little twigs (this is interest on your interest). Over the years, a single seed grows into a large, flourishing tree with numerous branches, all stemming from the original seed. Similarly, your initial investment grows over time through compound interest as the interest builds upon itself.

Morgan Housel describes how Warren Buffett built his fortune mainly through patience: $81.5 billion of his $84.5 billion net worth were accrued after his 65th birthday.[18] Warren Buffett may not be the most successful investor. He may just be the most patient one, ready to play the long game. He sits out numerous bull and bear markets, but benefits in the long run.

Historically, stocks or shares have yielded better returns than other investments over the long term. Yes, the stock market goes up and down, but over many years, it generally trends upward. This makes stocks a pretty solid option for retirement planning.

Saving is a commendable first step. Effective investing is what really multiplies those savings. Here are some basic principles to keep in mind.

Minimize costs: Opt for cost-effective savings plans and avoid trading apps. Focus on cost-effective and passive funds that mirror broad market indices and ensure that the ongoing costs, ideally, remain low. Even a large number of financial advisers would agree that these funds deliver a performance that is 'good enough' for most households.

Long-term vision: Consistency is key. Save regularly and automatically and resist the temptation to frequently check and adjust your portfolio. Daily, weekly, even monthly checking can lead to impulsive decisions, often driven by market panic or euphoria. (If you use an app for your long-term savings, be mindful that it will encourage more frequent checking of performance and/or pot size. And that, in turn, may trigger actions that drive bad outcomes for yourself.)

Personal goal-oriented investing: Set goals that are *important to you*. Research shows investors who focus on personal goals are more likely to stay the course, even in tough times, and achieve better long-term outcomes as a result.[19] Worry less about the economy and pay more attention to the lifestyle you aspire to.

Mortgages – Good or Bad?

A mortgage payment is more than just an expense; it's a form of 'forced savings.' A mortgage might initially seem like a heavy monthly financial obligation. However, another perspective could be that each payment not only covers the interest but also gradually increases your equity in the property. This approach transforms a monthly expense into a long-term asset. For many, it leads to financial stability and a deep sense of security.

Our financial wellbeing research at the Centre for Behavioural Research yielded interesting results: those who haven't paid off their mortgages by retirement or who rent are often financially constrained.

They have significantly less disposable income compared to those who are mortgage-free. That, in turn, more often results in real stress and anxiety for many. The financial buffer needed for a comfortable life is considerably larger for them compared to those who have paid off their mortgage.

Renting can be a great (and even more cost-effective) choice under circumstances where lifestyle and financial flexibility as well as mobility are important. I get Ramit Sethi when he suggests that there's a "pro-home-ownership propaganda" that discourages people to run the numbers on the biggest purchase of their lives.

"We are blind to running the numbers because in this country we have propaganda: 'Owning a home is the best investment you'll ever make. You're throwing money away on rent.' Funny, nobody ever said you're throwing money away at a restaurant. 'You're paying your landlord's mortgage.' Funny, you never seem to be concerned about paying your sushi restaurant owner's mortgage. But, suddenly, we use these almost-religious phrases when it comes to buying a house."[20]

As Sethi points out: for many people, especially those in high-cost urban areas, renting can be more practical than buying. Renting allows you to avoid the significant upfront costs of a down payment and maintenance expenses. It frees up funds for investments or other things and experiences that may be more worthwhile investments on your path to prosperity.

However, if you're considering staying put in a place for a longer period – ten years, say – then buying that property likely helps you recoup transaction and maintenance costs, build equity and have paid-off a mortgage by the time you want to slow down.

An overall conclusion I would draw from our research is that owning property is less about its contribution to your overall net-worth figure. The long-term emotional and psychological value it brings is immeasurable. So is the stress that having to pay rent or pay off a mortgage in retirement results in.

Given these insights, another rule of thumb is: aim to have your mortgage paid off by retirement age.

BRILLIANTLY SIMPLE: THE 50-30-20 RULE

Up to this point, you've received many rules of thumb for managing money in a 100-year life. Why all these rules of thumb? Why not something more concrete or specific?

The answer is simple. First, and rather obviously, I can't make statements directly tailored to you. That is to say, there may be better, more cost-effective or more profitable alternatives for you specifically in the long run. But here's the second point. The rules of thumb I've given you have been proven to be 'good enough' for the vast majority of households. Investing much more time, effort and cost into marginally better alternatives may not justify the actual added value.

There's a third reason: Rules of thumb tap into our natural, intuitive thought processes.[21] We know, of course, that we should budget. We constantly hear that we should accurately track income and check expenses, that we should thoroughly and honestly record ongoing fixed costs (like rent or mortgage payments, phone bills, car tax, gym memberships) and ongoing expenses (clothing, leisure, entertainment, holidays). Certainly true. But it's a bit like explaining to Homer Simpson that doughnuts are unhealthy. Factually correct. But will that knowledge really be implemented?

Rules of thumb acknowledge that we're not all Mr Spocks. Rather, we're more like Homer Simpson. They are easy to digest (the rules of thumb that is, not the doughnuts). They align with the cognitive tendencies of our brains.

To conclude the 'Money Chapter,' let's consider one more brilliantly simple rule of thumb: the 50–30–20 rule. It goes like this:
* 50% of your net income should be allocated to necessities.
* 30% can be spent on wants or desires.
* 20% should be set aside to improve your financial situation.

Here are a couple of examples:
* Let's say Robert earns £2,000 net per month.
* He spends £1,000 on rent, bills and groceries – ideally, life insurance and critical illness cover are also included in these fixed costs (50%).
* He spends £600 per month on leisure activities or a modest shopping spree (30%).

- The remaining £400 he uses for saving or paying off debts (20%).
- Tina earns £5,000 per month.
- She spends about £2,500 on her mortgage, car and other essentials (50%).
- She has around £1,500 left for holidays, tech gadgets or dining out (30%).
- And £1,000 she can use for savings or debt repayment.

You get the idea. It's really quite simple.

Elizabeth Warren, the US senator, and her daughter, Amelia Warren Tyagi, developed this rule of thumb in their book, *All Your Worth*.[22] They saw a political need for it because, in the past, banks, mortgage lenders, credit card companies and other financial institutions had to ensure their customers could afford their products. That's no longer the case today. The responsibility to ensure our financial lives are in order lies squarely with us. We're on our own! This can be overwhelming, frustrating and difficult. But simple rules of thumb can help.

Regarding the last 20%, consider what your priority might be: if you're struggling with high-interest debt (like credit card debt), use the 20% to pay down debt. If you don't have an emergency fund, use that 20% of your income to build it. Once you've eliminated your pressing debts and have an emergency buffer, you should contribute to the transition fund with the 20% of your net income. And, of course, they should also flow into retirement savings.

From time to time, take a moment to determine what portion of your income you spend on necessities, what portion on desires, and what portion you use to improve your financial situation. Is it about 50–30–20? Or is it more like 50–25–25? Or 40–30–30? There may be good reasons for the latter scenarios. Perhaps you've just come out of a period of unemployment and need to rebuild your transition fund. Or you're only now, in your mid-40s, realizing that you haven't started saving for retirement privately. Then, deviating from this rule of thumb is worthwhile. But there might be other reasons. Ask yourself why you think deviating from 50–30–20 is right. What does that say about you and what's important to you?

We'll revisit the 50–30–20 rule later on. I'll explain why I think it's a clever way to handle the complex trade-offs we need to make in a 100-year life.

THE 50-30-20 RULE WITH ANNA AS AN EXAMPLE

How could our rule of thumb help my friend, the filmmaker Anna, mentioned earlier in the chapter?

Anna's situation illustrates a common dilemma: the pursuit of personal fulfilment in a creative profession while simultaneously needing financial security. Her dedication to her craft and her refusal to compromise for commercial success are admirable. But here's perhaps the core problem: She's far from 50–30–20. She calculates and says it's more like 70–25–5.

While Anna has no debt, she also has no savings – neither for emergencies nor for transitional phases. She has almost nothing set aside for retirement. Anna's desire to avoid compromises is understandable on the one hand. On the other hand, it poses a risk to her long-term financial wellbeing. For Anna, as for anyone navigating a multistage life, it's crucial to find a balance between pursuing talents, interests and values on one side and ensuring financial security on the other. Integrating some of the discussed principles – like aiming for an income that is 'good enough,' the importance of savings for emergencies and transitions, and planning for later life – would provide Anna with a more stable foundation for both the present and the future. It would also allow her to continue her creative journey without the constant fear of financial instability.

The old distinction of the 'true' and the 'false' self by psychologist Donald Winnicott is helpful when we think about the balance of financial security and personal fulfilment. More about this can be found in Winnicott's book, *The Maturational Processes and the Facilitating Environment: Studies in the Theory of Emotional Development.* This theory can help us understand how we can balance our inner world with external demands. We should acknowledge that we have a true self. A self that represents our true feelings and desires. But there is also a false self. A self that helps us navigate the social and professional world and accept certain things. Maybe we find a colleague's suggestion fundamentally ridiculous (says the true self). But we say, "Sure, great idea," and just go along with it (through the false self).

Anna lives very much according to the needs and desires of her true self. However, she risks her long-term financial wellbeing by refusing to allow a false self. We can all probably understand this somehow. I'm not always my true self in the professional world either. There are things that frustrate me. I could make a fuss. But if it wouldn't help anyone, I put my true self in check and act through my false self.

Accepting both aspects of the self leads to greater self-understanding and compassion for ourselves. It allows us to maintain genuine relationships while effectively operating in our broader social and professional world. For Anna – and all those whom Anna, here, represents – this means acknowledging and integrating both her passion for filmmaking (her true self) and the necessity of financial security (an aspect of her false self). Perhaps she might find ways to maintain her creative integrity while also achieving some financial stability. I wonder if Anna has fully explored if there are other opportunities to earn more money without compromising her artistic vision. Perhaps there are ways to align her talents with financial stability that she hasn't considered yet. Balancing her true self and her false self isn't easy, but it's worth thinking about – especially in a world where financial security is so tightly linked to long-term wellbeing.

———————

SIGNPOST

Imagine you're sitting in a luxury hotel, let's say in Dubai. You're reclining in an oversized, plush chair, taking in your surroundings. Above you, a high ceiling adorned with a chandelier sparkling like a sea of stars. On one wall, there's a massive aquarium filled with exotic fish in every colour of the rainbow. Next to it, there's a group of statues that look like they've stepped straight out of ancient mythology. Between the statues, a man-made waterfall gently cascades.

A small robot rolls up to you. It balances champagne glasses on a tray. It stops and offers you a glass with mechanical precision. You take it, sip and breathe deeply. You smile. And you start to ponder a few questions:

- When would I accept a standard as 'good enough?' (Think about the things necessary for your daily wellbeing.)
- What monthly income is 'good enough' to meet my basic needs and some of my wants?
- Is there a point in my career where I've reached 'good enough'? What marks this point?

- What are the intangible aspects of my life that are already 'good enough' and couldn't be improved by more money?
- How do I define 'good enough' regarding my work-life balance? What's the optimal balance for me?
- When is my living situation 'good enough?' What aspects are crucial for this feeling?
- Looking back, what aspects of my childhood can I consider as 'good enough?'
- In which areas of my life do I already feel I have more than 'enough?' How do I manage that?
- What kind of holiday would be 'good enough' for me?

Let's take a moment to review the key points from this chapter:
- We've recognized that money matters. On your path to prosperity, it's a crucial *ingredient* for success.
- To support this, we need an income that's 'good enough.'
- Debt should be managed carefully, ideally keeping debt payments below one-third of our total pre-tax income.
- It's wise to keep three months' salary aside as emergency savings – or, for households, three months of combined income.
- An additional six months' worth should be set aside in a transition fund.
- A retirement savings plan is essential, as is following the 50–30–20 rule for financial management.

If these steps are set up and automated – like paying off debt, building emergency and transition funds and saving for retirement through direct debits or salary deductions – then managing your personal finances shouldn't take more than 30–45 minutes a month.

By doing this, you've not only organized your finances but laid the foundation for prosperity, allowing you to focus on other things – importantly, the things that bring happiness and meaning to a long life.

Having learnt all this, let's move on to Money Mindset.

CHAPTER 3

THE BALANCE IN YOUR HEAD: MONEY MINDSET

Let's begin this chapter with a quiz.

What share of the UK public do you think understand the importance of having emergency funds?
  A) 23%
  B) 51%
  C) 88%

What share of the UK public say they understand the necessity of planning and adhering to a budget?
  A) 27%
  B) 48%
  C) 87%

And what portion is aware that they need to plan financially for retirement?
  A) 21%
  B) 42%
  C) 78%?[23]

If you voted like most people I conduct this quiz with, you most likely chose A) or B) for all three questions.

The correct answer for each, however, is always the last one: C.

Surprised? Let me state it this way:

- 88% of people in the UK know that it's important to have emergency savings.
- 87% understand that they need to manage their income and expenses sustainably.
- 81% of them are aware that they need to save for retirement.

Do you understand?

The point, of course, is this: just because people are aware of something – or just because they know it rationally – doesn't mean they will act on that knowledge. In fact, there's plenty of evidence that people behave as though they don't know these things: many people have no savings.[24] Many are in debt.[25] And according to many studies, the amounts saved for the long-term is far too low.[26]

Why don't people act in the way they *know* they should? Maybe because they can't? Maybe because they objectively can't afford to save? Because they can't avoid accumulating debt? Or because they don't have the means to prepare for retirement?

This may be the reason for some. As previously stressed: money is important. Without money, many things become difficult.

But mindset also plays a role, too. The balance in your bank account is important. But just as important is the right balance in your mind.

In this chapter, we'll explore what influences the right balance in your mind.

OF ATTITUDES, BELIEFS
AND EMOTIONAL REACTIONS

Becoming aware of our attitudes, beliefs and emotional reactions is already a significant step forward. Do any of the following sound familiar to you?

ATTITUDES

Attitudes toward money shape how we make our financial decisions. Each of us wears a set of lenses that shapes our view on money and finances.

Take, for instance, risk aversion. This perspective often leads to prioritizing security over growth. People with this attitude tend to favour safe investments like savings accounts, even if they offer low returns. In the long term, this likely means building fewer savings than what might have been possible with a more balanced approach to risk. Here, the opportunity for financial growth might be missed.

Some people are more optimistic, especially when it comes to financial prospects. They invest in new ideas and ventures, often without fully considering the associated risks. Their optimism can lead to financial setbacks, as they might overlook the necessity of having a safety net.

Entitlement is another attitude. Someone with a strong sense of entitlement might feel they deserve financial success without significant effort – believing that a comfortable lifestyle should come naturally or that others (employers, family or the government) should provide for them. This attitude influences spending, saving and career choices, often leading to frustration when reality doesn't align with expectations.

These three examples illustrate how our attitudes toward money influence our financial behaviour. An imbalance in these attitudes can prevent us from saving and investing effectively. They can also prevent us from enjoying a good life today.

"I prefer shopping at a budget supermarket rather than an expensive one and saving the difference for my retirement" – this is an attitude where present-day comforts are sacrificed for the success of the future self. This isn't inherently bad, especially if there's no other way to save for the future. But the nonmonetary price of this attitude for the present self might be too high, too.

BELIEFS

Let's now look at beliefs. Beliefs about money are deep convictions that influence our attitudes and decisions regarding finances. These beliefs are often shaped by personal experiences, cultural influences and family upbringing.

One common belief is, for example: Money brings happiness. People who internalize this belief tend to seek happiness in material possessions and may live beyond their means. They might struggle to keep their spending in check because they are convinced that more money will inevitably lead to more happiness.

Another belief is the notion that financial success is mostly a matter of luck or fate. This conviction can lead to a passive approach to financial management. People with this belief often think that their financial situation is mainly determined by external circumstances, neglecting the aspects that are within their own control.

'Financial struggles are a normal part of life' – another widespread belief. People who think this way often see debt as unavoidable and feel powerless to improve their financial situation. This mindset can trap them in a cycle of financial problems and debt.

Beliefs differ from everyday attitudes toward money. The latter are more superficial reactions to financial situations. Beliefs, however, explain why we act the way we do. They are the 'whys' behind our financial decisions.

Beliefs can also ruin a pleasant 100-year life: the belief of a 35-year-old that one should strive for the next pay rise now because "these are my productive years" internalizes a three-stage life, where productive years and times of living off savings are tied to age. The story of Dr Ingmar Zöllner – the trained eye doctor who became a train driver – is perhaps so impressive because he questioned the belief that one should aim for early retirement at the end of a career rather than taking new risks.

It's easy to judge others and say their approach to money is crazy. We see people who go into debt for big weddings, buy lottery tickets, invest in risky stock, or spend excessive amounts on hobbies. And we quickly think such decisions are irrational. But it's much harder to recognize that behind this consumption are deep-rooted beliefs about money.

Take, for example, people who go into debt for a large wedding celebration. For many, this decision reflects not just personal values but cultural expectations as well, where a grand wedding is seen as a meaningful way to honour love and commitment. They may feel that such an event justifies the financial stretch, especially when cultural traditions and family expectations are at play. In this view, certain life events carry unique importance, making them worth the investment, even if it requires financial sacrifice.

Is that crazy?

I don't think so. I believe that people act in ways that make sense to them at the moment, shaped by their personal beliefs, cultural influences and desires. Every decision has an internal logic that's completely valid to the person making it. "No one is crazy,"[27] as Morgan Housel nicely puts it, "including ourselves." We all carry our respective beliefs about money with us.

But it's worth reflecting on these beliefs, as they can sometimes nudge us toward financial choices that stray from our other, mostly long-term goals. By understanding the deeper values and cultural influences behind our spending, we gain the freedom to make deliberate choices – deciding which traditions to embrace and which to reshape to serve our own vision of a prosperous life.

EMOTIONAL REACTIONS

Emotional reactions to money are another crucial component of our money mindset that is worth developing an understanding for. They encompass spontaneous and intense feelings that arise in financial situations and significantly influence our behaviour. These reactions can feel both positive and negative, ranging from joy and relief to anxiety and stress.

For example, the joy of an unexpected pay rise can lead us to make optimistic and sometimes careless spending decisions. On the other hand, the stress triggered by receiving a large bill can lead to overly cautious or even fearful behaviour. Such emotional reactions are not only immediate and intense but also have long-term impacts on our financial planning and decision-making.

Another powerful emotional reaction is envy, which can be triggered by seeing a colleague receive a pay rise or scrolling through social media and noticing friends enjoying expensive holidays or luxury purchases. Envious feelings can lead to financial decisions driven more by comparison than necessity – such as overspending to "keep up" or feeling demotivated about one's own financial progress. Left unchecked, envy can contribute to impulse purchases, financial dissatisfaction, or even riskier financial behaviour in an attempt to match others' perceived success. Recognizing these triggers and their impact is key to maintaining financial decisions that align with personal values rather than fleeting emotions.

A typical example where emotional reactions play a role is private retirement planning. Although many people rationally understand the necessity of saving for retirement, emotional barriers such as fear or feeling overwhelmed, shame or avoidance prevent them from taking appropriate actions. The fear of not saving enough or the complexity of financial planning can be paralyzing. Similarly, a mindset of denial or indifference toward retirement can lead to procrastination or complete avoidance of the necessary steps to secure financial stability.

These emotional reactions are often deeply rooted. They reflect our fundamental attitudes and beliefs about money. They might stem from past experiences or familial influences. Either way, they have a strong influence on our financial behaviour and our short- and long-term financial success.

To develop a healthy money mindset, it's important to become aware of these emotional reactions and develop strategies to manage them.

Carl Jung, the Swiss psychiatrist and psychotherapist, captured it perfectly: "Until you make the unconscious conscious, it will rule your life, and you will call it fate." Each of us has internalized certain beliefs, developed specific attitudes and formed habitual reactions to money. None of these are inherently good or bad – they can be helpful or limiting, depending on how they influence us.

Take the belief that 'a penny saved is a penny earned.' This can be helpful because saving is one of the most powerful ways we have to build long-term financial security. But if saving becomes the sole focus, it might come at the expense of enjoying life in the present or meeting your immediate needs and wants. Similarly, a frugal attitude can be positive when it helps avoid waste or unnecessary expenses. Yet, taken too far, it might lead to missed opportunities for meaningful experiences or investments in yourself.

Emotional reactions also play a double-edged role. For instance, a touch of anxiety might prompt you to check your bank account regularly and stay on top of your finances. But if that anxiety spirals into constant worry or avoidance, it can cloud your ability to make thoughtful financial decisions.

Or take envy: we often think of envy as a purely negative sensation. Something to suppress or avoid. The common advice is to simply "stop comparing yourself to others." But that's unrealistic. Comparison is deeply human. We gauge our success as parents, colleagues, and individuals in large part by observing others. Whether it's evaluating our salary, work-life balance, relationships, or even health, we rely on comparison to make sense of where we stand. The goal, then, can't be to eliminate comparison but to compare more wisely.

Instead of seeing envy – or any other emotional reaction – as a destructive force, we can use it as a tool for self-reflection. The next time you feel envious – whether it's over a friend's promotion, a bigger house, or a more flexible lifestyle – pause and ask yourself: what's behind this feeling? Wanting a higher salary or a different lifestyle isn't inherently bad, but digging into these emotions can reveal deeper insights. Is the envy signalling a real misalignment in your life, or is it just a fleeting reaction? If it points to something meaningful – like a desire for more autonomy, better financial security, or personal growth – it can serve as a powerful motivator to refine your goals and take constructive action toward a more fulfilling financial path.

We will explore the role of emotions in a successful 100-year life more closely in the second part. For now, let's note: your money

mindset has been shaped by the people, environments and circumstances you've encountered – factors that may look very different
from the reality you live in today. On your path to prosperity, it's
essential to recognize and examine these inherited attitudes, beliefs
and emotional responses closely. By understanding and learning to
talk about (for example, with your partner) what serves you and what
doesn't, you gain the clarity and freedom to reshape your approach to
money in a way that supports the life you want to live.

OF INNER CHIMPS AND BIASES

At the beginning of this chapter, there was a quiz. Most find the correct answer surprising: even though many people *know* what would
be right, they often don't *act* as though they would. This raises the
question of whether financial education is necessary at all. It's a political question: many governments place a high value on financial education and spend a lot of money on corresponding campaigns.

The answer is a clear "yes." Yes, we need financial education. But
we need a different kind of financial education. One that not only
conveys technical and functional knowledge but also helps us understand how our mindset influences our financial decisions.

In the following sections, we will dive deeper into understanding
our inner biases and how they affect our financial choices.

THE 'INNER CHIMP'

I'm sometimes asked how I teach my eight-year-old twins the right
way to handle money. My answer: we don't talk about money that
much. We talk about the 'inner chimp' – a concept from Steve Peters.[28]
The inner chimp symbolizes the emotional and impulsive part of our
brain. It reacts quickly, often without deeper consideration, driven by
emotions and instincts.

Here's how it works with my kids: when they insist they need
more sweets after dessert, or beg for extra TV time instead of

winding down for bed, we say, "That's not you, that's your inner chimp." When they get grumpy because their sibling is having too much fun with a favourite toy, I remind them it's their inner chimp getting jealous, not their true self. And when they're tempted by every shiny new thing in the store, we explain it's their inner chimp drawn to the sparkle, not a real need. By recognizing their inner chimp, they start to see the difference between impulsive urges and thoughtful choices.

This concept of the inner chimp is, of course, based on Daniel Kahneman's distinction between System 1 and System 2 thinking.[29] System 1 is our fast, intuitive and emotional thought process, while System 2 is slower, more deliberate and logical. Daniel Kahneman, originally a psychologist, became a central figure in behavioural science. Let's look at some key concepts from behavioural science that shape and influence our money mindset.

Understandably, we tend to choose the path of least resistance, especially when it comes to financial decisions. Using System 2, our slow and logical thought process, is exhausting. It's like trying to navigate through thick fog – doable, but laborious. It requires concentration and caution. Therefore, it's hardly surprising that we often shy away from using it. System 1, our fast and intuitive thinking system, is always active. It works quietly in the background and influences our decisions without us realizing it. It's like an autopilot guiding us through the day. This system prefers the easy, effortless way. It relies on familiar patterns and habits, avoiding anything that requires effort or discomfort.

Here are three examples.

- When driving home from work or another regular destination, System 1 often takes over. We might think about other things or listen to music while driving, yet we still arrive home without actively thinking about each turn or action. Our brain has navigated this route so many times that it's become second nature.
- When shopping, we often grab the same products without consciously thinking about it. Our choices are guided by long-standing preferences and habits. We might always buy the same brand of bread or milk simply because that's what we've always done, not because we're making a conscious decision each time.

- In social interactions, we often respond automatically with standard answers like "I'm fine, thanks" when asked "How are you?" without really thinking about how we actually feel. These automated social courtesies are deeply ingrained in our behaviour and are controlled by System 1.

Each of these examples show how much we rely on our fast, automatic thinking in daily life. System 1 is not bad. In fact, it's a crucial part of our cognitive toolkit. Without System 1, our daily lives would be unbearably complicated and exhausting. Imagine having to consciously think about every little action, every step and every decision. It would lead to cognitive overload and significantly impair our ability to function.

System 1 allows us to respond quickly and efficiently to our environment. It's responsible for intuitive judgments and automated reactions that are not only helpful but often essential for survival. For example, when we instinctively sense that someone is untrustworthy based on subtle cues, or when we quickly avoid a risky situation without needing to analyse it in detail.

This system is the result of a long evolutionary development. It helps us recognize patterns and respond quickly to familiar situations without our brain having to go through the energy-intensive process of conscious, analytical thinking every time. In many everyday situations, these fast, intuitive decisions are not only sufficient but often the most effective way to act.

The challenge, however, is to recognize when we can rely on our intuitive thinking and when we should pause and switch to System 2, our slower, reflective thought process. This is especially important in complex situations where hasty decisions can lead to suboptimal outcomes in the distant future.

In the world of finance, unreflective reliance on System 1 can lead to impulsive purchases, neglect of long-term goals or disregard of important information. Therefore, it's crucial to find a balance between the fast, intuitive power of System 1 and the slower, more deliberate analysis of System 2. This is a key part of a successful money mindset.

BIASES

The 100-year life presents unique challenges for financial planning and life management. It requires a longer period of financial self-sufficiency, meaning we must accumulate sufficient resources for healthcare, lifelong education, and potential career changes. But financial planning is not just about saving; it involves making constant trade-offs between present enjoyment and future security. Balancing short-term wellbeing with long-term stability requires ongoing adjustments, as decisions made today shape both our financial resilience and overall quality of life in the decades ahead.

Various cognitive biases influence how we prepare for a long life – or fail to prepare.

The Myopia Bias, also known as short-sightedness bias, describes our tendency to give more weight to short-term goals rather than long-term ones. In the context of a 100-year life, this means we often prioritize immediate needs and desires over long-term planning and saving. We tend to make decisions that bring instant gratification, even if these decisions could jeopardize our long-term financial security. This bias leads us to underestimate the importance of early planning and investing in our future, whether it's regarding career, family, health or retirement.

The challenge is to envision the distant future and perceive it as real and urgent. We generally pay more attention to what's directly in front of us – the next days, weeks or months. Long-term goals, like saving adequately for a 100-year life or investing in our continuous personal development, often seem less urgent. We postpone important decisions and actions because they don't bring immediate benefits in the present.

The Optimism Bias makes us see the world through rose-tinted glasses. We tend to overestimate the likelihood of positive events in our lives while underestimating potential risks. In financial planning, especially when planning for a 100-year life, this bias can be dangerous. It leads us to assume we need to save less because we expect to stay healthy, work longer or simply get lucky. This overly optimistic attitude can leave us unprepared for challenges like unexpected health expenses or changes in the job market.

The Status Quo Bias makes us stick to our current situations, even when changes would clearly be beneficial. This is particularly relevant when considering that a 100-year life requires a flexible, adaptable mindset. People with a strong status quo bias might struggle to rethink their financial strategies, pursue career development or make necessary lifestyle changes. They stick to familiar patterns and decisions, even if these aren't optimal for a long and fulfilling life.

These biases are just a few examples from a vast pool identified by behavioural scientists. They illustrate why planning for a 100-year life is so challenging. It's less about rational difficulties – we understand the challenges at hand rationally. The real challenge is mental. It lies in our money mindset.

OF SCARCITY MINDSET
AND 'SLACK'

To have the right money mindset for a prosperous 100-year life, it's essential to understand and manage the 'scarcity mindset.' This concept is a central theme in the book by renowned economist Sendhil Mullainathan and leading psychologist Eldar Shafir, *Scarcity: Why Having Too Little Means So Much*.[30] They explore how the feeling of scarcity – whether it's time, money or other resources – restricts our cognitive capacity and makes us focus on the immediate and scarce.

The problem: this narrow focus on scarcity pushes other equally important matters into the background. This so-called 'scarcity trap' keeps us in a state of constant short-term crisis management at the expense of long-term perspectives and solutions.

THE SCARCITY MINDSET

We could see a scarcity mindset in action during times of high inflation or the so-called 'cost of living crisis.' During this phase, our attention often zeroes in on rising prices. We'd go to the bakery and notice that rolls had become more expensive yet again. The same went for butter, dishwasher tablets, gifts for the kids and so on. In times of high inflation, it's hard not to focus on whether or not things have become more expensive. This has immediate consequences: we might shop less or buy cheaper alternatives or take measures like having shorter showers and turning down the heating. These actions will help reduce costs. They are understandable and can help. They fulfil an immediate need for financial relief.

What's the problem? The narrow focus on scarcity risks trapping us in a scarcity mentality. This mentality makes us only concerned with immediate problems, neglecting the bigger picture. The bigger picture is that this period of high inflation is just one of many events that happen in our longer, healthier lives. I think it's important to be aware that everything happening here and now is part of a longer life span. In fact, that's the big challenge of our time. Every financial decision we take – earning, spending and managing related – doesn't just affect the present but also the long-term future. We must remember that we are living longer, even if times are tough today.

One side note: behind the headlines reminding us of the cost-of-living or whatever other financial crisis, I think there's a bit of naïve optimism, too. It somehow suggests that we live in a world where prices should remain stable. It fails to accept that there have always been times of inflation and deflation. Ironically, preparing for a happy 100-year life also means being somewhat pessimistic or fatalistic: it's inevitable that we'll experience crises.

In the previous chapter on money, we discussed the need for emergency funds and transition funds. These are financial resources that help us in tough times. But they do more than that. They don't just plug financial holes. They give us 'slack.'

UNDERSTANDING 'SLACK'

'Slack' is the extra mental space and resilience that comes from having a buffer against life's inevitable challenges. Emergency savings or transition funds are the tangible financial resources. Slack is the freedom in your mind that follows: the mental bandwidth to handle what life throws at you without overwhelming stress.

Slack isn't just about having money in the bank; it's about the peace of mind that comes from not living paycheck to paycheck. It's the mental relief of knowing that you have savings to fall back on for several months if needed, that your credit cards aren't maxed out, and that your budget has some breathing room for unexpected expenses.

When you have slack, you're empowered to make choices from a place of strength rather than urgency. You can take time to find the right job instead of accepting the first offer out of necessity. You're not stuck in a cycle of crisis management, choosing between essentials. Instead, you're equipped to plan for both your immediate needs and your longer-term goals, building a future where you can both survive and thrive.

With emergency savings, transition funds, fewer costs on needs and the willingness to dial down on needs when necessary, you build slack into your financial approach. By preparing for life's inevitable bumps, you can reduce stress, make more considered decisions and cultivate a sense of freedom and resilience throughout your 100-year life.

In fact, slack is particularly relevant in a 100-year life. A scarcity mindset, focused on short-term survival strategies, can prevent us from fully embracing the opportunities of a longer life. It can make us stay in jobs we dislike just to pay the rent or stop us from taking time for preventive health measures like going to the gym. Slack – or more mental bandwidth – enables us to think beyond the day-to-day and be more proactive in shaping our long-term lives.

SIGNPOST

Imagine you're travelling through France. It's a warm autumn day. By chance – maybe a recommendation from the owner of the last B&B or the woman standing behind you in the queue – you find yourself visiting a local monastery. You wander through the monastery's halls, appreciating the serene atmosphere. Your footsteps echo softly.

You reach a courtyard and notice that, despite the lovely weather, there are only a few other visitors around. You look for a place to sit and find a spot on the edge of a fountain in the middle of the courtyard. Your gaze sweeps across the area. You take in the symmetrical architecture, exuding calm and stability. The lovingly maintained flowerbeds and gardens, perhaps preserved for centuries, remind you of the monks who once lived here in contemplation. You sit and start to reflect on yourself and your own beliefs.

Which two of the following keywords best describe your view on money?
- Freedom
- Responsibility
- Power
- Happiness
- Security
- Burden

Now, imagine these five different money personalities:
- The Saver
- The Spender
- The Investor
- The Indifferent
- The Generous

Rate each personality on a scale of 1 (that's not me at all) to 5 (that's exactly me).

Here are five popular beliefs about money. Rate each belief on a scale of 1 (I strongly disagree) to 5 (I strongly agree):
- Money is the root of all evil.
- Money provides security and stability in life.
- Money corrupts character.
- Money can make dreams come true.
- Money is not important for happiness.

———————————

We close the first part here.

Hopefully, some key points have become clear in this first part:
- We need money. Without money, things get tough. Specifically, we need an income that is 'good enough.' We need reserves for emergencies. We also need reserves for transitional phases. For longer time horizons, we need savings plans in diversified portfolios. Property plays a role. It's worth getting into debt for the latter. Such debts are okay if they go into items that have a realistic chance of gaining value in the long term. Debt is bad if it is used for things that tend to lose value. The 50–30–20 rule helps us balance all this.
- But money isn't everything, nor is knowledge about managing it. Equally important for financial success is understanding our attitudes, beliefs and emotional reactions – and recognizing their helpful and limiting sides. Without this awareness, as Carl Jung noted, we may simply view our financial outcomes as fate.

- The concept of financial wellbeing acknowledges both sides – money and mindset. It's not just about the balance in your bank account but about the balance in your head. This is what distinguishes financial wellbeing from the pursuit of financial independence, which often assumes that a certain amount of money alone brings happiness. The Buddenbrooks, however, show us that this isn't always the case.
- The Buddenbrooks, like many who chase wealth, believed that money – having it, earning it, sustaining it – was the key to a successful and happy life. But remember the ingredients metaphor? A good life requires money, yes, but it also needs other essentials. Just as bread needs more than just flour, a fulfilling life needs more than just money. Proponents of financial independence often see wealth as the key ingredient for happiness but overlook the compromises made along the way. Like the Buddenbrooks, they sometimes pay for financial independence with strained family ties, neglected relationships and missed opportunities for the experiences that truly bring life meaning. They may grasp the benefits of material wealth but miss the deeper value of prosperity – where money provides not just security but also the freedom to live a life rich in purpose and connection.

I'll admit it – I get wound up by some of the self-proclaimed experts preaching their clever tricks and hacks for achieving financial independence. The truth is, it's not that easy to get there with stocks and shares, rental property, bitcoin or whatever else they're selling. Most of those preachers were just lucky. They'll say it's about having the right money mindset, but let's be honest: mindset isn't some magical ability to imagine goals into reality. As Daniel Crosby put it so well, you can be financially successful and still be a moron.[31] And "trust yourself" is really bad money advice.[32] What's more important is understanding where your money mindset comes from and how it drives your decisions – good or bad.

But even that's not enough. Mindset alone doesn't build financial security – what matters is how it translates into action. A sound financial approach isn't about clever tricks or shortcuts; it's also about patience, and making decisions that align with your values. Investing doesn't have to be complicated – low-cost index funds or target retirement funds, for example, provide broad market exposure without the need to outguess the market. Patience matters because long-term growth requires sitting through uncertainty. And, perhaps most importantly, financial success is personal. It's not about someone else's definition of prosperity, but about saving consistently, maintaining flexibility, and making trade-offs that support your own priorities.

Maybe I shouldn't get so caught up in calling out the financial independence preachers and their gospel of positive money mindset. After all, money has a way of making all of us act a bit strangely. It's confusing. And planning financially for a 100-year life? That's next-level confusing.

Let's unpack that in the second part.

PART 2

Evolution and Emotions: Mastering Money

Our species, Homo sapiens, has been around for about 300,000 years.

If you were to tell the entire history of humanity in one calendar year, our ancestors would have first appeared in East Africa on January 1. And right now, it would be just before midnight on December 31.

January	February	March
Mo Tu We Th Fr Sa Su	Mo Tu We Th Fr Sa Su	Mo Tu We Th Fr Sa Su
1 2 3 4 5 6 7	1 2 3 4	1 2 3 4 5
8 9 10 11 12 13 14	5 6 7 8 9 10 11	6 7 8 9 10 11 12
15 16 17 18 19 20 21	12 13 14 15 16 17 18	13 14 15 16 17 18 19
22 23 24 25 26 27 28	19 20 21 22 23 24 25	20 21 22 23 24 25 26
29 30 31	26 27	27 28 29 30 31

April	May	June
Mo Tu We Th Fr Sa Su	Mo Tu We Th Fr Sa Su	Mo Tu We Th Fr Sa Su
1 2	1 2 3 4 5 6 7	1 2 3 4
3 4 5 6 7 8 9	8 9 10 11 12 13 14	5 6 7 8 9 10 11
10 11 12 13 14 15 16	15 16 17 18 19 20 21	12 13 14 15 16 17 18
17 18 19 20 21 22 23	22 23 24 25 26 27 28	19 20 21 22 23 24 25
24 25 26 27 28 29 30	29 30 31	26 27 28 29 30

July	August	September
Mo Tu We Th Fr Sa Su	Mo Tu We Th Fr Sa Su	Mo Tu We Th Fr Sa Su
1 2	1 2 3 4 5 6	1 2 3
3 4 5 6 7 8 9	7 8 9 10 11 12 13	4 5 6 7 8 9 10
10 11 12 13 14 15 16	14 15 16 17 18 19 20	11 12 13 14 15 16 17
17 18 19 20 21 22 23	21 22 23 24 25 26 27	18 19 20 21 22 23 24
24 25 26 27 28 29 30	28 29 30 31	25 26 27 28 29 30
31		

October	November	December
Mo Tu We Th Fr Sa Su	Mo Tu We Th Fr Sa Su	Mo Tu We Th Fr Sa Su
1	1 2 3 4 5	1 2 3
2 3 4 5 6 7 8	6 7 8 9 10 11 12	4 5 6 7 8 9 10
9 10 11 12 13 14 15	13 14 15 16 17 18 19	11 12 [13] 14 15 16 17
16 17 18 19 20 21 22	20 21 22 23 24 25 26	18 19 20 21 22 23 [24]
23 24 25 26 27 28 29	27 28 29 30	25 26 27 28 29 30 [31]
30 31		

Humans settle down
Humans invent money
Humans invent retirement

Around 70,000 to 80,000 years ago, (so, sometime in October), our ancestors left Africa and spread across the globe. Until about 12,000 years ago – around December 13 in this yearly analogy – they lived as nomadic hunter-gatherers. The average lifespan rarely exceeded 30 years. Around December 13, we settled down. We began to cultivate land. This led to the foundation of the first civilizations.

About 4,000 years ago, on December 24 of our metaphorical year, the first money-like artifacts and coins started circulating.

And it was only 150 years ago, symbolically around 6 pm on today's New Year's Eve, that our modern concept of retirement took shape.

Given this perspective, it's no wonder that the demands of a long life can sometimes feel overwhelming. In the grand sweep of human history, we're simply beginners at the art of crafting a long life.

In this section, we delve into the evolutionary challenges that arise when planning for a century-long life.

CHAPTER 4

STONE AGE THINKING: WHY MANAGING MONEY IS SO HARD

It might seem absurd that something like a money mindset even exists. Why do silly things like emotions, beliefs, attitudes and instincts get in the way of the right financial behaviour? After all, we are Homo sapiens. We are not monkeys, kangaroos or penguins. We're not even Homo neanderthalensis, Homo erectus or Homo habilis.

We are Homo sapiens. This literally means 'wise humans.'

We gave ourselves this name to emphasize our ability for complex thinking and significant intellectual development compared to other species. 'Homo sapiens' captures the unique cognitive abilities of humans: reason and the ability to create complex cultures and technologies.

The other human species that inhabited this planet with us thousands of years ago might have been strong. They may have had unique abilities to adapt to their environments. But we are the ones who thrived and evolved. The others died out.

In this chapter, we go back to the hunter-gatherer times of our ancestors. I don't know what names people gave themselves back then, so let's call them 'Adam' and 'Eve' for simplicity.

The world of Adam and Eve and their daily lives were, of course, very different from ours today. They lived in small nomadic groups of about 150 people. They were constantly on the move, searching for food, water and shelter. Their lives were dictated by the seasons and the availability of resources. This led them to follow the migration patterns of the animals they hunted and the growth cycles of the plants they gathered. Their sweetest joys were ripe fruits. Imagine Eve coming across a patch of juicy, wild strawberries. She immediately fetches Adam, and they enjoy them together, knowing that if they don't, the nearby cave bears would quickly devour the berries.

This instinct to quickly consume high-calorie and sweet food was a crucial survival trait back then. It's still deeply embedded in our DNA today. That's why we devour chocolate bars, ice cream and other sweets just as eagerly as Eve did with the strawberries. It's a prime example of how we still possess the same physical, emotional and cognitive characteristics as our ancestors from thousands of years ago. But, while certain instincts served them well then, they often no longer do so today. In the days of Adam and Eve, longevity wasn't even an option. There was no need to consider the long-term consequences of poor diet choices. Similarly, there was no need to save for the future. Today, we constantly must weigh the present against the future. Our natural survival tactics from the past often don't align with today's necessities. No wonder we find it overwhelming.

EMOTIONS AND REASON
NOW AND THEN

We tend to think of cognition, motivation and emotion as separate entities. For instance, when we say, "Set your emotions aside and look at this rationally." But this separation doesn't work. Cognition involves all the processes that happen when we think and perceive – our thought processes and information processing in the brain. Emotions are our experiences of feelings, which can be both intense and subtle. Motivation is the drive that moves us to act.[33] These three elements are closely intertwined and influence each other in our daily experiences. They're part of the same operating system.

From a neuroscience perspective, the interplay between cognition and emotion is more intricate than it might seem. Two key brain regions involved in this process are the prefrontal cortex and the amygdala, which are part of a broader network regulating thought and emotion. The prefrontal cortex, particularly the dorsolateral region, is responsible for higher-order thinking, reasoning and impulse control. The amygdala, a key structure in the limbic system, plays a central role in processing emotions, especially those linked to threat and reward. These regions are deeply interconnected, creating a dynamic feedback loop where emotions shape how we perceive and judge situations, while cognitive processes can regulate emotional responses. As a result, our decisions are rarely purely rational or purely emotional – they emerge from the continuous interaction between these systems.

Fear, curiosity, envy and hope are examples of emotions that don't exist in isolation from cognition and motivation. They are integrative experiences that influence our perception, thinking and actions. For example, fear can serve as a warning signal, prompting us to think and act more cautiously. Curiosity opens us up to new ideas and fosters creative problem-solving. Hope can enhance our resilience and motivate us to keep going despite difficulties and challenges. Envy can highlight desires or unmet goals, prompting reflection on what matters to us.

It's not always that emotions come first, and cognition and motivation follow. Often, the process begins with a rational thought or a motivated action that then elicits emotional responses. This emotional feedback can, in turn, influence our cognitive processes and decisions. Emotions can be seen as an additional perspective in decision-making. Like a team where different viewpoints and expertise come together, emotions provide valuable information and insights that complement purely cognitive considerations.

Take a job offer, for example. You might start by rationally analysing the pros and cons of the offer. The prefrontal cortex is active in the logical evaluation of the situation. Simultaneously, the amygdala plays a role by bringing in emotional responses like fear of change, curiosity about new challenges and hope for career improvement into the decision-making process.

You see, emotions are by no means mere disturbances of rational thinking. They are an integral part of our cognition and motivation. They enrich our understanding of the world and might even be the reason we think and perceive in the first place. Emotions are not just side effects of our thoughts and actions; they are essential elements that shape our experiences and behaviours.

This is true today, and it was true thousands of years ago. It's a part of being human. Let's briefly consider how this interaction of emotion, motivation and cognition might have played out during our hunter-gatherer years.

Adam and Eve lived in a nomadic group of about 150 people. Their lifestyle was marked by constant movement in search of food and resources. They lived in close harmony with nature and were dependent on their environment, which influenced their daily activities and decisions. One day, their group encountered unfamiliar tracks while wandering. The unclear threat triggered fear. This emotion led to caution. The group decided to avoid the tracks and choose a safer path. The motivation to seek safety for their group directly followed from the fear and the resulting cautious thinking.

On another occasion, they came across an unknown plant. The curiosity of some group members was piqued. Driven by this emotion, they explored the plant further, despite the risk involved. Their cognition, stimulated by curiosity, led them to consider whether the plant might be edible. Some decided to try it.

When a drought threatened their food sources, hope became the driving force. Hope enabled Adam, Eve and their group to keep going despite the difficult circumstances. It motivated them to seek new food sources and influenced their decision to venture into unexplored areas in the hope of finding water and food. At the same time, envy may have played a role – seeing another group with more abundant resources could have sparked a drive to improve their own situation, pushing them to adopt new survival strategies or migrate to more fertile lands. In these examples, emotion comes first, followed by action and rational consideration.

But emotions don't always come first. Sometimes, Adam and Eve made rational decisions first, like choosing a longer but safer route to avoid predators. After making their decision, they felt a certain fear of the dangers they might still encounter. This fear heightened their vigilance and caution during the journey.

In the group, Adam and Eve logically considered the possibility of developing new tools to make hunting more efficient. This cognitive deliberation resulted in heightened curiosity about what might be possible with the new tools. The curiosity motivated the group to experiment with different materials, leading to innovative new tools.

In all scenarios – whether emotion first or cognition first – the complex interplay of emotion, motivation and cognition in the daily lives of our ancestors thousands of years ago is evident. Their decisions and actions were shaped by both their emotional responses and their rational considerations. This interplay allowed them to survive dynamically and adaptively in an ever-changing environment.

THE INVENTION OF MONEY – A TURNING POINT IN HUMAN HISTORY

Our hunter-gatherer ancestors didn't have money problems because they didn't have money. That's why the emotions we associate with money today only appeared in different contexts for them. Our ancestors didn't fear unemployment; they feared wild animals. They didn't regret not having built financial cushions earlier; they might have regretted not stockpiling enough for the winter or missing a good hunting opportunity. Lack of retirement savings was not a cause for shame. Shame might have stemmed from violating social norms or betraying the trust of the community.

FROM BARTER TO DEBT

The common belief is that early economies relied on barter – trading goods directly, such as a basket of apples for a pair of shoes. But anthropologist David Graeber challenged this view. In his book,

Debt: The First 5000 Years,[34] he argues that our understanding of the history of money is fundamentally flawed. According to Graeber, the essence of money lies not in coins, notes or other physically tradable items. Indeed, while our ancestors didn't have 'money' in tangible forms, they had a complex network of obligations that held their communities together. They didn't necessarily trade a basket of apples for a pair of shoes. However, within their nomadic groups, there was a sort of division of labour and cooperation. One person might be skilled in healing, while another was adept at weaving, providing clothes for others. If someone helped build a house, they could rely on the favour being returned at harvest time. In short, there weren't necessarily direct, immediate trades, but there was a system based on mutual trust, obligations and communal reciprocity. Economically speaking, it was a system of debts and credits maintained over time in the collective memory of the community.

In our nomadic communities, we didn't have money. But we were still rational and emotional beings. Therefore, we likely experienced what we would now recognize as 'money emotions': the fear of not contributing enough and thereby losing the community's support, the curiosity to explore new ways of cooperation and exchange, and the hope to survive and thrive through mutual assistance and collaboration. All of this was likely already present back then.

Even when we settled about 12,000 years ago, we still didn't use money for a long time. Contrary to the popular idea of a 'barter system,' early economies likely relied on systems of trust, reciprocity and mutual obligation within communities. In early cities like Jericho, exchanges may have involved grain, tools or labour, but these were often underpinned by social relationships and trust rather than simple trades between strangers. People supported each other's needs and kept promises because of the bonds within their community. This system likely fostered an early money mindset, shaped by concerns about providing for families, hopes for improving life through cooperation and the shared ambition of building a secure and thriving community.

THE IMPACT OF MONEY ON OUR LIVES

Then, around 4,000 years ago, something significant happened – something we're still grappling with today.

We invented money.

Sometimes, when I have a bit of time before catching the train back to Edinburgh, where I live with my family, I visit the British Museum near Kings Cross Station. I head to rooms 68 to 73 and explore the treasure troves that reveal the history of money. More specifically, I explore the history of money when we reduce it to coins, notes or other physically tradeable items. This exhibition, featuring metals, shells and intricately crafted objects, spans over 4,000 years of human history. It showcases the role money has played in shaping our world.

The first exhibits in these rooms show that, long before the advent of jingling coins or shimmering gold bars, civilizations valued various other materials as 'exchange mediums.' Visitors are invited to imagine the markets of ancient China, dominated by vibrant jade, bronze goods and the artful beauty of cowrie shells. These weren't just trade goods. No, they were coveted status symbols, tangible proof of wealth and influence. Back in those days, a family could trade highly prized cowrie shells for all sorts of household necessities. And a merchant could receive bolts of luxurious silk for a piece of exquisite jade.

Adjacent to the Chinese collection are artifacts from Egypt. These hint at early monetary systems that testify to trade and wealth. A photo of a mural from a tomb in Thebes from 3,400 years ago shows gold rings being weighed on a scale. Temples back then were not only places of worship; they were financial centres managing weights and, later, meticulously documenting payments and loans. A document from 1823 BCE describes a silver loan between a temple and a citizen, complete with repayment terms and interest rates.

We learn that as early as the 3rd millennium BCE, silver in Mesopotamia was not just a shiny metal but a highly valued centrepiece of many transactions. Fun fact: if you bit someone's nose in a fit of rage, you owed them half a kilogram of silver. It paid to keep your instincts in check even back then. These and other curiosities are recorded in the ancient Babylonian legal code of Eshnunna, written on two clay tablets, which also listed ideal silver prices for basic foodstuffs.

Egypt, with its wealth of gold from Nubia and the abundant agricultural gifts of the Nile, was a land of plenty. A letter from that time even claims that gold was as plentiful in Egypt as dust. The Egyptian monetary system was fascinatingly flexible. A policeman who needed an ox could partially pay with copper and settle the remaining amount with goods like fat or clothing.

These two ancient civilizations, Mesopotamia and Egypt, were pioneers in establishing standards of value. They facilitated not only local trade but were also crucial in long-distance commerce. However, it was the Lydians (from Lydia, in what is now Turkey) who get the credit for inventing coins as we know them. Using electrum, a gold-silver alloy, they created coin-like objects, even some with inscriptions. This marked the beginning of organized coin minting. It is no wonder that the last Lydian king, Croesus, who ruled from around 555 to 541 BCE, is still a symbol of wealth today.

This journey, from humble shells through radiant jade to the first coins, reveals the fascinating development of early monetary systems. It highlights the complex interplay between value, trade and social foundations. As our ancestors recognized the importance of a standardized medium of exchange, they laid the groundwork for today's complex economic infrastructures.

MONEY EMOTIONS AND
THE ART OF MASTERING THEM

The introduction of formalized money systems likely clashed with the older mindset shaped by trust, reciprocity and mutual obligation that had guided exchanges for thousands of years. I wonder what the first mental money challenges people faced back then were?

Unfortunately, there's no record of this – at least not in the British Museum. It's quite possible, however, that many people, just like today, had fears about the new and unknown. The introduction of money was a radical change, and the resulting anxiety likely stemmed from its abstract and impersonal nature. Previously, life had been built on systems of trust, reciprocity and mutual obligation, where value was tied to tangible goods or relationships. Some probably struggled to understand the concept of assigning fixed values to coins or tokens and, out of fear of being cheated, may have clung to familiar forms of exchange until they adjusted. Perhaps these emotions created challenges at the time – or maybe they offered valuable lessons for navigating this new way of life.

I can easily imagine that many others were fascinated by the possibilities that money offered. They began experimenting with different types of trade, opening up new avenues for commerce and wealth building. This curiosity was likely a catalyst for the development and acceptance of money as a medium of exchange.

Hope certainly played an important role too. The idea that money could simplify trade and lead to more security and prosperity was enticing. This hope, that money could enable them to live better lives, surely encouraged many to take the risk and integrate money into their economic system, even if the transition was initially daunting.

During this period of change and development, people's emotional and cognitive processes were put to the test. Their reactions to the new phenomenon of 'money' reflected these emotional states. Fear likely led to caution in handling money, while curiosity and hope motivated the exploration of new economic pathways. This mix of fear, curiosity and hope, along with many other emotions, likely shaped how early societies made financial decisions. It may have also shaped many of the confusions and inconsistencies we still observe and feel today.

Yuval Noah Harari, in his beautiful book, *Sapiens: A Brief History of Humankind*,[35] examines the concept of money and its evolution over time. He identifies one of the crucial turning points in the evolution of money as its detachment from tangible value. Initially, money – in the form of coins, shells or other metals – was directly tied to tangible items of inherent value. For example, in the past, coins were linked to commodities like grain: a coin represented a fixed amount of grain, its value was thus intrinsic and concrete, and it could always be exchanged for its equivalent in grain. This system was based on the physical and tangible, on things you could touch, see and directly use.

As societies grew, such a 'tangible' system became cumbersome. It would have been impractical to carry the exact grain equivalent for every purchase or to store vast amounts of grain to back every coin in circulation. It was a system with clear limits. At this point, what Harari describes as a massive mental revolution began.

Over time, we started placing our trust in abstract concepts. Coins, and later banknotes, began to represent value. They weren't objectively worth that amount. The actual metal or paper of the banknote had only minimal inherent value. But we *believed* they were worth it. And we acted accordingly.[36] This mental revolution allowed for greater economic fluidity and scalability. Currency could now be easily produced and transported and used for a wide range of transactions without being burdened by the need for a direct physical equivalent.

But perhaps we can also trace the roots of many of today's mental challenges related to money back to the mental revolution of that time. Harari's explanation of the transition from tangible to abstract forms of money reveals the mental challenge that the proper handling of money poses for us. No wonder we have various, and often contradictory, beliefs, mindsets or emotions about money:

- "Money can't buy happiness."
- "More money, more problems."
- "Money makes the world go round."
- "Time is money."
- "Money is the root of all evil."
- "The best things in life are free."
- "Save for a rainy day."
- "It takes money to make money."
- "A penny saved is a penny earned."

If money doesn't have a tangible or objective value, it opens up a lot of room for interpretation and emotional reactions, heavily influenced by our individual experiences, cultural backgrounds and social contexts.

Nowadays, as cash becomes less relevant, this process of abstraction is even more pronounced. Cashless transactions mean we trust the balance shown on our banking app and believe we can buy this or that. Sellers, in turn, trust that they can sell us all sorts of goods when our plastic card makes that satisfying beep on the reader. My eight-year-old twins love to tap my card on the reader. They find the beep incredibly rewarding. But I do wonder how I can explain the value of money and the need to earn it when all they need to do to buy groceries and other things is to wave a plastic card at a machine.

Although we understand rationally that we need to earn money, save up, handle debt carefully and prepare for retirement, the complex interplay of emotion and cognition makes this difficult. The development of money into an abstract medium of exchange has complicated matters further: money often exists only as a number on a screen, far removed from the tangible reality our ancestors dealt with.

This abstraction of money means our emotional and cognitive reactions to it become more complex and sometimes contradictory. We struggle with the emotional burden of debt, the fear of financial insecurity and the hope for financial freedom. At the same time, our cognitive thoughts influence how we save, invest and spend money.

The common advice to make financial decisions purely rationally and save emotions for other areas of life is unrealistic. Emotions, cognition and motivation are tightly interwoven and always influence our decisions. We can't simply 'switch off' emotions when dealing with money. They are an integral part of our thought processes.

A more effective approach to dealing with emotions is to recognize and name them. As Gill Hasson explains in *Emotional Intelligence: Managing Emotions to Make a Positive Impact on Your Life and Career*, emotions are not inherently wrong or irrational. They have an evolutionary background and often serve a positive intent, even today. For example, fear can protect us from danger, and excitement can drive us toward opportunity. However, emotions can sometimes get in the way, especially when it comes to achieving good long-term financial outcomes. By acknowledging and understanding our emotions, we can manage them more effectively, ensuring they guide rather than overwhelm us in moments of decision.

Brené Brown, known for her research on vulnerability and shame, aims in her book, *Atlas of the Heart*, to explore and name common emotions. Her goal is to develop a better understanding of our emotional reactions and thus enable a more conscious handling of them. Let's look at a few emotions from Brown's book and how they might affect us in financial matters:

- Fear can prevent us from taking career risks or investing in opportunities that promise higher returns.

- Shame might make it difficult for us to talk about our financial situation, complicating debt management.
- Envy can lead us to make impulsive purchases to keep up with others, rather than planning long-term and saving.
- Joy can drive us to make spur-of-the-moment buying decisions that don't align with our long-term financial goals.

All emotions have the potential to hinder the right financial conduct if we don't recognize and manage them properly. The solution lies in becoming aware of the emotions guiding our financial behaviour. We should acknowledge their strengths and dangers and learn to talk about them with our partners, friends or acquaintances. More and more financial advisers and coaches are learning to discuss money emotions. An open dialogue about our emotional reactions to financial topics can help us develop better strategies for dealing with money and ultimately lead to healthier financial decisions.

I don't have any
money for this
nonsense. I've got to
save for retirement.

It's OK to be
scared of the
future. But, I also
have a life today.

SIGNPOST

You're taking a walk through a beautiful landscape. You see the fields and roads, thinking, "This must have looked similar 12,000 years ago." Back then, there were no power lines, no paved roads or marked hiking trails. The landscape was wilder, untouched – a mix of dense forests, open fields and rough paths, shaped only by nature and the animals living there.

But some things would hardly have changed over the millennia. The topography, the gentle hills on the horizon, and the babbling brook flowing through the valley – they were already there.

You wonder what it was like for people walking here 12,000 years ago.

Our relationship with money is based on instincts developed for a time when money didn't exist. What instinctive reactions do you have toward money? Are you a collector, a hunter, a preserver? How do these instincts influence your financial decisions?

Twelve thousand years ago, needs were simple: food, shelter, community. Today, they're more complex and often intertwined with money. List your basic needs and evaluate how money plays a role in them. Identify which needs are genuine and which are distorted by modern complexity.

- What emotions influence your approach to money? Do you feel secure when saving or free when spending? How might your financial behaviour be shaped by prehistoric survival instincts?
- Our ancestors relied on their community for safety and success. How does your social environment influence your relationship with money? Consider peer pressure, status symbols and communal financial decisions.
- Think of the modern economy as a 'financial wilderness.' How would you navigate this wilderness? Are you a bold explorer, a cautious observer or an adaptable wanderer?

To sum up: showing emotions in financial behaviour is not only normal but also inevitable. We are humans. We are emotional beings. Our decisions are always influenced by a combination of feelings, thoughts and physical reactions. Accepting this is the first step toward a healthier relationship with money.

People today possess the same emotional, cognitive and physical abilities as our ancestors. The crucial difference lies in our social and cultural context, which has drastically changed over the past millennia. Five thousand years ago, there was no money as we know it today. However, our instincts and emotions result from an evolutionary development spanning over 300,000 years.

This explains why many of us struggle to find the right way to handle money. It's not because we, as individuals, are incapable. The complexity and fast pace of our modern world challenge us. Our instinctive reactions, once vital for survival, aren't always helpful in managing the financial demands of the 21st century.

It's important to be empathetic and self-compassionate toward ourselves and not too harsh. Our financial challenges aren't due to personal shortcomings. They result from a deep discrepancy between our evolutionary makeup and the requirements of modern life.

In the next chapter, we'll examine how we've developed certain expectations about state pensions and the so-called three-stage life. We'll explore how these expectations came about and how we can best manage them. Because the problem is that the three-stage life is over, and the state pension isn't enough. This, too, is primarily a mental challenge.

CHAPTER 5

HABITUAL THINKING: WHY CARING FOR OUR FUTURE SELVES IS SO HARD

Until a few decades ago, there was little need to think much about funding retirement. Someone else usually had it covered – often the state through guaranteed pensions or social security schemes, or employers providing generous workplace pensions.

But in recent years, this has changed. The responsibility for securing our long-term futures now rests squarely on our shoulders. We're in charge.

The era when the safety net of a state-supported pension system was introduced is but a blink of an eye in human history. We only need to look back 150 years. Before that, all the way back to our ancestors Adam and Eve, there was no concept of 'retirement' and no planning for old age.

Adam and Eve lived, as illustrated in the previous chapter, in an immediate and direct relationship with their environment. When they needed shelter, they sought natural refuges like caves or built simple structures from branches and leaves. When they were hungry, they gathered edible plants or hunted. Their diet was based on what was available in their immediate surroundings. The concept of storing food or agricultural planning didn't exist yet. They ate what they found or caught, often right after harvesting or hunting.

When they were thirsty, they sought out water sources like rivers, lakes or natural springs.

Collecting and storing water for future use wasn't common. If they needed clothing or tools, they made them from materials available in their environment, like animal hides or stones. These items were crafted and used as needed. When faced with dangers like predators or natural disasters, they reacted immediately by seeking refuge or defending themselves. There were no long-term security strategies or prepared protection mechanisms.

The point is: there was never a need to think long-term. In almost every aspect of daily life, Adam and Eve focused on meeting immediate needs. Early humans lived in the here and now, without the possibility or necessity to plan for the long term. This essential focus on immediate rewards and needs contrasts sharply with the complex planning requirements of the modern world, including planning for retirement.

THE CONCEPT OF THE PENSION SYSTEM AND ITS PROBLEMS

Let's travel back to the year 1871. The newly founded German Empire was undergoing rapid industrialization. Cities like Berlin and Munich were expanding, with factories dotting the landscape. On one side, you had the grand buildings of wealthy entrepreneurs and aristocrats; on the other, the humble dwellings of the workers. Older people, in particular, were left out in the cold. Many had to keep working in factories, on farms or in coal mines well into old age, until their strength gave out. The sick, the infirm or the unemployed had to rely on family support or local charities. There were no state welfare benefits, no pensions, no social security. Life was exceedingly tough for large swathes of the population.

Meanwhile, the affluent elite lived comfortably, much like the Buddenbrooks. They had their estates, investments and savings. Servants catered to their needs. Their families often managed their wealth, ensuring a smooth transition into retirement.

But resistance was brewing. The working class across Europe was becoming politically active, demanding change. In Germany, the so-called social question had to be addressed by the government to avoid unrest and upheaval. Thus, in 1883, Chancellor Otto von Bismarck introduced social insurance, followed by the disability and old-age insurance in 1889. By 1891, the world's first state pension scheme was established: workers and employers paid into a state-managed fund, which promised pensions for older people. The aim was to provide financial security in old age, ensuring these people were not left behind.

Other countries followed suit. Austria, Switzerland, the UK, Ireland and many others soon introduced state pension systems. All these reforms had one purpose: to prevent poverty. They aimed to ensure that those without family or community support were not forgotten.

The welfare state was born. Rightly so! It promised hope. It tackled challenges. It changed society's view of older people. Better yet, there was optimism that this welfare state was here to stay, even to expand. While the initial goal was to ensure the basics, the welfare state gradually evolved into something that offered unprecedented safety nets.

Let's take a little time jump: after the hard years of the two world wars, much of Europe experienced a period of economic recovery and growth. Living standards rose, and consumer capitalism emerged. With new prosperity came new expectations for retirement. It was no longer just about being financially secure, it was about enjoying the pleasures of life that had been hard-earned.

In many Western nations, social democratic or Labour movements aimed not only to let retirees partake in economic growth but to actively support and enhance the living standards of those who had worked all their lives. This was more than political rhetoric. It was a societal metamorphosis. Economic growth, labour movements, political decisions – everything converged. Political campaigns mirrored this sentiment. Words like 'rights,' 'entitlements' and 'deserved' became everyday language. Gradually, the belief emerged: after years of work, the retirement years are the 'golden years.' For the well-heeled, cruise ship markets sprang up, offering tailored packages specifically for the retiree demographic. Retirement communities in beautiful locations flourished, offering a mix of recreational activities, healthcare and social events. Wellness retreats and specialized travel tours began targeting the older generation, promoting active lifestyles and cultural engagement.

To be clear, not all older people suddenly lived in luxury. For many, retirement is more about managing tight budgets rather than luxury cruises. Some have more money and can enjoy nice things. Others have less and need to be careful with their spending. However, as a group, people over 65 generally have more security and opportunities than ever before. Many enjoy their retirement with better health and more wealth, with social systems significantly contributing to this state. As a group, life satisfaction levels are highest for people in their early 70s, while anxiety levels decrease with age, too.

It made sense to introduce a state pension. And it's understandable and right to strive for a better life. But the state-supported retirement phase was a consequence and product of its time. It was introduced, institutionalized and normalized within a short time frame. What began as a mere safety net became a fixed, expected part of life, included in all plans and expectations.

Expectations take on a life of their own. This applies to retirement expectations, too. When people desired more security in old age, governments responded. Benefits were expanded, promises reinforced. This cycle, this feedback loop, strengthened beliefs and expectations.

Today, we face new economic pressures, a result of increasing globalization. We all know examples of companies moving jobs to China, Mexico or Serbia because labour is cheaper there. National economies are increasingly interconnected internationally.

Moreover, there are declining birth rates. In 2000, in wealthy countries, there were 26 people over 65 for every 100 people aged 25 to 65. By 2050, this number will likely have doubled.[37] Such trends naturally challenge the way state pensions are funded.

Another reason state-supported pension systems are challenged is the demographic development that came with the expansion of the welfare state: increasing longevity. Over the past 150 years, one of the most profound changes in human experience has been the dramatic rise in life expectancy. In many Western countries, average life expectancy has significantly increased over time. In 1870, it was about 40 years. By 1920, it had risen to about 55 years and further to about 71 years by 1970. By 2020, average life expectancy reached around 80 years. When Germany started paying out its first old-age pensions, there were just 126,000 souls who benefitted from it. Today, there are over 20 million.[38] This trend is seen in other industrialized countries, too. In the past, people in the UK who reached 100 years of age received a birthday greeting from the reigning monarch. Nowadays, you need to apply for it due to the high number of centenarians. In just 20 years, between 2002 and 2020, the number has nearly doubled.[39]

Alongside increased life expectancy, there has been an improvement in health: advances in medicine, sanitation, nutrition and public health mean that many diseases and conditions that once shortened lives are now preventable or treatable. We're not just living longer; we're living healthier and more vigorous lives.

Recently, some countries, including Germany, the UK and the US, have seen a slowdown in improvements in life expectancy.[40] Several factors contribute to this trend. Known reasons include the rise in smoking among women, the opioid epidemic in the US, and austerity measures in the UK.[41] There are also unknown factors that make understanding the overall issue complex.

However, in many nations like Italy, Japan, New Zealand, Norway and Switzerland, life expectancy continues to rise. Additionally, better-educated groups surpass the national average in terms of life expectancy. This suggests that in most countries, there is still significant room for improvements in longevity, provided that the positive economic and social forces that have driven life expectancy up since the mid-20th century remain stable.

As positive as longer life expectancy is, it puts national pension systems (and welfare systems in general) under pressure. In the EU, for example, the OECD (Organization for Economic Cooperation and Development) predicts that public spending on pensions as a percentage of GDP will increase by more than half. That's why recent political reforms tend to increasingly emphasize the growing responsibility of the individual. The state is increasingly pulling back and aiming to provide only a basic safety net. The rest ... well, it's up to you!

While this is the direction some policymakers are aiming for, attempts at such reforms often meet with strong resistance – particularly in Europe, with France being a notable example. The resistance isn't just about financial benefits; it's rooted in deeply ingrained beliefs. People are not only fighting for benefits but also defending long-held expectations. A 2023 survey conducted in Germany highlights these expectations:[42] a large majority (63.4%) want to retire at the age of 63. More than a third even want to retire at the age of 61 or earlier. Fewer than 15% of those under 30 can imagine working until the age of 67. These hopes and desires are understandable. But they also illustrate that pension policy is not just an economic challenge. It's also very much about managing expectations. And this is where we, as individuals, come in. The way we think about work, ageing and financial security shapes not only our own future but also the broader system we rely on.

RETIREMENT AND ITS MENTAL CHALLENGES

Letting go of established expectations is never easy. For many, one of the most deeply ingrained expectations is that life after work will be simpler, slower and more financially secure. The mere thought of considering alternatives – such as working longer or taking more responsibility for long-term financial security – can feel overwhelming or even disappointing. Yet, this shift in thinking is becoming increasingly necessary.

Historically, there is no precedent to guide us through the complexities of longevity. The concept of retirement, as we understand it today, is a relatively recent invention, developed over the last 150 years. For most of human history, people worked until they were physically unable to do so. Spending decades in leisure after a career is something neither our biological nor cultural ancestors prepared us for.

From an evolutionary standpoint, our brains are not designed for retirement. Our ancestors thrived in environments that required immediate action and gratification for survival. Long-term planning and delayed gratification – both essential for successful retirement – run counter to this ingrained wiring. While modern society has shifted to include planning for tomorrow, the challenge is magnified today as people live longer and traditional safety nets, such as state support, are being scaled back.

Beyond the inherent challenges of long-term planning, retirement itself often proves to be more mentally challenging than anticipated. A key issue for many is the question of identity and self-worth. Work is far more than a source of income: it provides purpose, structure and belonging. Retirement often means losing this sense of identity and recognition, which can lead to feelings of uselessness and the loss of a social role. As Riley Moynes describes in his four phases of retirement,[43] many retirees enter a phase of disenchantment, struggling to adjust to this new reality. Retirement coaches (an emerging profession) frequently observe how this can lead to existential crises, despite retirement being the culmination of years of effort and planning.

Adjusting to a new routine is another common struggle retirees face. After decades of structured work life, the absence of clear obligations can create feelings of aimlessness. Yes, there's a period of travelling, perhaps, or a lot of time on the golf course in year one. But after a while, the newfound freedom, ironically, often leads to boredom and a lack of purpose. Without the challenges and achievements that work provides, retirees must learn to navigate the 'trial and error' phase Moynes has identified, experimenting with activities and roles to rebuild their sense of meaning and identity.

Financial insecurity further compounds these mental challenges. Even those who have saved objectively healthy amounts may experience anxiety about whether their resources will last. Many financial advisers observe that it's hard to turn habitual savers into happy spenders. Potential later-life healthcare costs and the uncertainty of longevity only heighten these concerns.

Social and emotional challenges are equally significant. Losing the camaraderie of colleagues can lead to loneliness and isolation, requiring retirees to actively seek new ways to maintain relationships.

The absence of natural social interactions from work makes this a critical focus for a healthy retirement.

Perhaps counterintuitively, extended retirement might not even be as beneficial for health as once thought. Studies have linked early retirement to cognitive decline, underscoring the importance of staying mentally and socially engaged.[44]

"Every financial services company feels like they need to take a picture of a couple sitting in beach chairs and looking out over the ocean," says Michael Finke in Christine Benz's interview series.[45] "And have you done that?" he asks.

"I've done that before. I've sat by the ocean and just looked, and I can last maybe an hour. Maybe I'll read a book. But by the time I get to the end of the week, I'm done. I'm ready to do something different. And when it's just a vacation, it's glorious to be on a beach where it's warm, and to be doing something different than the regular grind. You appreciate the change in your routine.

"But when the leisure activity becomes the routine, is it really going to provide the same amount of satisfaction as it used to when it was the thing that you did when you were on vacation, or the thing that you did on the weekends?"[46]

Retirement is not just about freedom and leisure – it's a complex transition that demands thoughtful preparation and a clear vision of what a good life looks like in this phase (or rather 'its different phases'). It's important to visualize your in-retirement lifestyle – not just in financial terms, but in how you'll spend your time and maintain purpose and structure. Retirement shouldn't be seen as one long weekend or perpetual vacation, as Finke questions in the quote above. Without a plan for meaningful activities and habits, the lack of structure can lead to aimlessness and dissatisfaction. Future retirees must anticipate potential pitfalls by establishing routines, prioritizing health and relationships, and embracing purposeful activities that align with their values. Whether it's working in a reduced capacity, volunteering or pursuing hobbies, the goal should be to create a retirement that balances leisure with purpose. By taking a proactive and flexible approach, retirees can ensure this chapter of life is not only financially secure but also rewarding and meaningful.

FROM A THREE-PHASE TO A MULTISTAGE LIFE

Understanding that retirement is a recent invention has a crucial implication: it shows us that we can think about it differently. But how?

You've already read about the concept of the 100-year life several times. This idea, developed by psychologist Lynda Gratton and economist Andrew Scott, represents more than just a demographic shift. It's not primarily about whether we will live to 100 years old, but rather that we are generally living longer and healthier lives.

The key point is this: the 100-year life means a life with multiple phases. It's no longer a rigid three-phase model but a dynamic multistage life. Here's a more detailed explanation:

With the establishment of the pension system in the last 150 years, the notion of a three-phase life has solidified. Our lives have been divided into three clear-cut stages: education, working life and retirement. This model provided us with order and structure and became the norm over just a few generations.

Today, this model has become more fluid, though. Some of the reasons for this have been highlighted in the stories at the beginning of this book. In the story of Ingmar Zöllner, the former eye doctor who now works as a subway driver, we see that many of us no longer want to stay in the same line of work our entire lives. Emily, the freelance writer now serving sparkling water, shows us that rapid changes in industries can *force* us to pursue new career paths because our previous jobs become obsolete. It's not our choice. And in the case of Martina, who asks, "Mum, when will you finally die?" it becomes clear that longevity brings new challenges, such as caring for an elderly relative.

Added to this are the economic challenges of drawing a pension for 20, 25, 30 or even 35 years. Living longer means needing more financial resources. These funds need to come from somewhere, especially as the state increasingly steps back.

As a result, the traditional three-phase model of life is proving to be increasingly inadequate. It often fails to align with our personal aspirations and is unsustainable in the face of current macro-social and macroeconomic changes. So, how should we reconceptualize retirement to better fit our evolving lives?

Here's an answer inspired by Gratton and Scott.

Retirement, as we know it, is evolving. It's no longer seen as an abrupt end to working life but rather as a phase you ease into. And just as easily, you can ease out of it – whether by choice (because you feel like earning money again) or necessity (because 'financial independence' in retirement isn't guaranteed).

In his latest book, *The Longevity Imperative*,[47] Andrew Scott invites us to a thought experiment. He asks, "Would you like more time?" And further, "If you had one extra hour per day, what would you do with it? If you had one extra day per week, what would you do with it?" It's likely you'd have many ideas about how to use that extra time. So why don't we think the same way about the 100-year life? Why do we tend to allocate our available time in a manner that was established 150 years ago?

We don't have to switch abruptly from full-time work to full retirement; instead, we can adopt a more fluid transition. This can be achieved by gradually reducing working hours, taking on new projects or engaging in consultancy work after the main career. Additionally, contemplating more breaks during what's traditionally considered the productive phase – such as sabbaticals or other forms of recreational time – can provide valuable opportunities for rejuvenation and personal growth.

While taking extended breaks isn't a luxury everyone can afford, the benefits of integrating meaningful pauses into our careers are substantial. Given that our working lives may extend to support longer, healthier lives, embracing recreational times – whether it's taking the whole summer off to spend with your children, pursuing a beloved hobby or simply stepping back to recharge – allows us to focus on what brings joy and purpose. These moments help deepen connections with family and personal interests, ensuring that we prioritize what truly matters amid the rush of daily life.

Moreover, these breaks play a crucial role in reshaping our financial habits by teaching us how to spend thoughtfully rather than just save. Many retirees struggle to shift from accumulating wealth to enjoying it. By intentionally taking periods where we stop earning and instead invest in experiences or passions, we can develop healthier spending habits and gain a better understanding of what makes us happy. These intentional pauses not only provide immediate personal benefits but also help us transition into retirement with a clearer sense of how to balance financial security with meaningful living.

There's a darker argument in favour of taking longer breaks during our careers.[48] Even though we live longer, healthier lives *as a group*, doesn't necessarily mean that you, dear reader, will reach 100 years old. Statistically speaking, one in 20 of my readers in the UK will die under the age of 50; one in ten under the age of 60; and one in four under the age of 70.[49] It's a sobering thought, but the point is this: you may not live as long as you hope. Perhaps it's unwise to delay all gratification in pursuit of a good life later, at the expense of your present self.

On a brighter note: should we live beyond 70 and get closer to 100, these recreational periods help you build an archive of beautiful experiences – memories of time spent with loved ones, adventures pursued and simple joys appreciated. These moments may serve as a foundation for gratitude and perspective, something we may look back on happily in later years.

Of course, there are practical challenges to this idea. Employers have to agree to more flexible work arrangements. In the UK, for example, an often-unused benefit is parental leave. Eligible parents can claim up to 18 weeks of unpaid leave per child until they're 18 years old. This provision allows parents to take extended time off – for example, for extended breaks. In my experience it's underutilized, perhaps due to the fact that it's unpaid holidays and the associated financial constraints. But in my experience, also, many simply don't know they have that option.

Similarly, taking breaks in our working lives requires financial resources. This is where transition funds (discussed in the money chapter) come in: they are designed to help make these periods possible. If you've built such a fund, don't wait for permission from anyone to use it.

Next, let's think about age and ageing.

AGEING IN OUR SOCIETY

Never before in human history have we lived as long as we do today. This brings a huge mental challenge. During our hunter-gatherer days, life was dictated by the laws of nature. Survival was a daily battle against the elements, predators and diseases. In this era, which spans from about 12,000 to 300,000 years ago, the average life expectancy was a mere 33 years.[50] This figure isn't just a statistic; it represents a life story drastically different from today. People in this era experienced rapid life cycles: a very brief childhood, a slightly longer phase of adulthood and then a swift descent into the end of life. Their entire existence revolved around immediate survival needs, leaving no room for thoughts about a distant future.

Around 12,000 years ago, we began farming and living in larger, settled communities. This fundamentally changed our relationship with the environment and each other. This progress came at a cost. As people started living closer together, infectious diseases found a fertile ground. Life expectancy at birth may have even slightly decreased during this phase.

During the ancient civilizations of Rome and Greece, philosophy, democracy and art flourished. Yet, despite this cultural richness, life was often harsh. Life expectancy was still only about 20 to 30 years, heavily influenced by the fragility of early life. Many children never reached adulthood, and the survival of each newborn was uncertain. Those who survived the dangers of youth often lived into their 50s and 60s, often belonging to the societal elite. Many had slaves and servants.[51]

The same was true in medieval Europe. The lives of those we associate with castles and knights were precarious, often shortened by disease and poor living conditions. Only those who survived the challenges of youth could experience a relatively extended life.

Jump to the 19th and 20th centuries. This era saw unprecedented advances in science and medicine and a seismic shift in life expectancy. Innovations in medical science, improved sanitary conditions and better nutrition rewrote the script of human life. By the early 20th century, the average life expectancy had risen to about 50 years. Most people could now expect to survive childhood, reach adulthood and even enjoy years beyond that. It was a time of transformation. The prospect of living longer began to imprint itself on the collective consciousness, changing the structure and expectations of society.

Today, in the late 20th and early 21st centuries, we stand on the brink of a new age. For the first time, living beyond 80 is the norm, not the exception. This remarkable increase in years is the result of ongoing improvements in healthcare, nutrition and a significant reduction in infant mortality. For today's generations, living to 100 is not a rare wonder but an achievable reality. We live in a world where ageing goes beyond mere survival, offering decades of potential growth, learning and contribution.

The mental challenge today is no longer about the fight for survival. It's about defining what it means to live a good, meaningful life over an extended period. This shift in life expectancy, from the fragile brevity of antiquity to the robust length of the modern era, sets the stage for a profound re-evaluation of ageing. It challenges deeply rooted perceptions and attitudes that have developed over millennia.

Ageing is often seen as a loss, a descent and a farewell to the bloom of youth. This notion is deeply embedded in our words and culture. Everyday expressions reflect this view. Phrases like "not as young as you used to be," to be "over the hill," and "put out to pasture" are not just words. They are powerful metaphors that shape how we see ageing. They suggest that it's more about retreat than continuing the journey of life.

The anti-ageing industry amplifies this narrative. It feeds on our fascination with youth. Ads and media are filled with messages that exalt youth, presenting it as the pinnacle of beauty, energy and significance. Older people are often shown in roles that focus on their decline, depicted as if they need to battle ageing rather than experiencing it as a natural, valuable phase of life.

This perspective extends into healthcare. Elderly care often focuses solely on age-related problems. Too frequently, the emphasis is on decline. The potential for continued growth and wellbeing is frequently overlooked. Discussions about improving mental, physical or emotional health in older age are rare. This creates an image of ageing primarily associated with the loss of abilities.

In the workplace, experienced workers often face age discrimination. They're seen as less innovative because of their age or aren't considered for certain projects. Job advertisements frequently call for 'vital,' 'flexible,' or 'energetic' new hires. This focus appeals to younger people, leading to older candidates being overlooked for these opportunities. To many older workers, it feels as though it potentially undervalues their experience and limits diversity in the workplace.

However, change is slowly emerging. Charities advocating for age inclusion are working to alter societal attitudes. They combat age-related stereotypes and promote the value of older workers. Their aim is to create a work environment where experience and age diversity are seen as strengths. Increasingly, companies are allowing former employees to register as senior experts and share their expertise with younger colleagues. At technology company Bosch, this includes 2,400 employees worldwide.[52] Other companies are enabling retired employees to return to work. Older individuals can participate in trainee programs just like younger ones.

This shift in attitude is essential. By recognizing the value of older individuals, both in the workplace and in society, we can create a more inclusive and supportive environment for everyone. It's about changing the narrative from one of decline to one of continued contribution and growth.

HOW TO THINK ABOUT AGE AND AGEING

The novel *The Seven Husbands of Evelyn Hugo* by Taylor Jenkins Reid gives readers a look into the life of a famous (but fictional) Hollywood actress. Evelyn Hugo spends many years chasing fame and beauty. The book follows Evelyn's rise to stardom, her seven marriages, and how she balances her public image with her personal struggles. As Evelyn looks back on her life, she shows the pressure women feel to keep up their appearance in a society that often values youth. Through her story, readers see the long-term sacrifices made for beauty, and how it affects personal relationships and self-identity.

Evelyn Hugo's relentless obsession with maintaining her beauty and youth is a central theme in the novel. Her meticulous grooming, glamorous image and strategic marriages are all parts of her calculated effort to stay relevant in the entertainment industry. The issue? Her obsession with youth comes with profound long-term consequences. Evelyn often prioritizes her appearance over her long-term wellbeing. It leads to strained relationships and a sense of regret for not pursuing what mattered to her. Her fixation on beauty serves as a facade that hides her vulnerabilities.

Ageing is, of course, a universal experience. But the societal emphasis on beauty and youth often results in a greater focus on women's appearance. The global market for anti-ageing products stood at around $47 billion USD in 2023.[53] It is expected to increase to nearly $80 billion USD by the beginning of the next decade. Approximately 70–80% of the anti-ageing market is driven by female consumers.

Susan Sontag, the photographer, author and cultural critic, delved into the societal pressures surrounding ageing in her 1972 essay, "The Double Standard of Aging."[54] She highlighted how women are burdened by the expectation to maintain their youthful appearance. Unlike among men, this expectation is leading to a persistent sense of inadequacy as they age. Sontag shared her own discomfort with ageing in this essay. She described feelings and beliefs of her worth diminishing with each passing year. Her insights revealed the personal struggles she faced as a woman and how they are rooted in societal norms and expectations, making it a collective issue rather than just an individual concern.

What has this got to do with long-term financial and life planning?

There's a significant gap in retirement savings between men and women. There's a number of objective reasons for this: the pension gap often stems from a mix of wage differences, career breaks (often due to childcare or caregiving responsibilities) and part-time work. In many countries, these factors contribute to women accumulating fewer retirement savings compared to men, which in turn leads to greater financial insecurity for women in later life.

It's clear: you need money to save for retirement. So, a gender pay gap eventually leads to a gender wealth gap. As we've seen before, money is important, but it's not everything. Mindset is crucial, too. And I suspect that some of the approaches we currently have to age and ageing might not be so helpful for long-term success.

Let me explain.

Remember the point we discussed earlier about the scarcity mindset? That's a finding from economists and psychologists Sendhil Mullainathan and Eldar Shafir. They found that when people are preoccupied with one thing, they find it harder to pay attention to something else. They've shown that when you have little money, you're so focused on making ends meet that you can't plan for the future. And as a result, you're less likely to save or invest. They've also shown that when you lack time, you become overwhelmed and less likely to engage in important tasks. Or that if you feel you lack friendship, you might neglect building new relationships.

Similarly, if we fear the visible signs of ageing and pay a lot of attention to preventing them, this preoccupation might crowd out our ability to think about our long-term needs and future selves. Simply put, when too much mental energy is spent on maintaining appearance, there's less bandwidth to focus on financial planning and securing a stable future.

There's more: we know that when we have a positive and intrinsically motivated connection to our future self, we're more likely to act in favour of that future self. Your future self, however, is – guess what – older than you are now. If instincts like fear of ageing and emotions like shame and denial prevent you from thinking about your older future self, then you're less likely to be able to sympathize and empathize with your future self. You'll find it hard to empathize with your future self's hopes, fears, requirements and needs. This avoidance can lead to real negative financial consequences.

In a trial we conducted at Aegon UK with the University of Edinburgh, we let men and women literally see a version of their future self. Through their computer's camera, their face was recorded and visually aged.[55] Simply put, their future selves looked a little like their present selves, only with more grey hair and wrinkles. When we explained to the study participants that this intervention was supposed to help people visualize their future selves and encourage them to save for retirement, many women in the group said something to the effect of "that only encourages me to take Botox."[56]

More generally, we know from our research that negative emotions like shame, regret and being overwhelmed reduce the likelihood of engaging with tools that help people plan their long-term finances. It makes sense: why would we like to engage in something if it makes us feel bad?

Taken together, this suggests that it's important to develop a different mindset and approach to ageing for long-term success. Instead of feeling pressured to maintain youth, we'd benefit from strategies that balance present wellbeing with future wellbeing – there'll be a place for some of the cosmetic products as a result. But by expanding the conversation around ageing beyond youth preservation to include holistic personal and financial development, we can help create a more balanced approach. An approach that supports both present wellbeing and long-term financial security. This alone won't close issues like the gender wealth gap. After all, structural and societal factors play a significant role. But adopting a more relaxed perspective on age and ageing can perhaps pave the way for a more financially resilient and fulfilling future.

Youth vs. Age

Back in the day, early behavioural scientists were often quick to label human behaviour as irrational. In their quest to challenge standard economic thinking – which assumed that humans are rational, cost-benefit-calculating homo economicus – they may have overemphasized biases and seemingly irrational behaviour. Today, we take a more measured approach, recognizing that what appears irrational in one context may make sense in another.

Many of our instincts, emotions and cognitive shortcuts – apparent biases, fallacies and illusions – may have had adaptive value. The obsession with beauty and youth, for example, might be deeply ingrained because, in ancestral environments, it helped guide complex long-term decisions under uncertainty. Some studies from evolutionary biology and psychology suggest that these preferences, while not necessarily optimal today, may have once played an important role in survival and reproduction.

From an evolutionary standpoint, youth is associated with fertility and reproductive potential. Consequently, we are subconsciously driven to choose partners who are likely to contribute to successful reproduction. This is particularly evident in men's preference for younger women, as fertility in women is more directly linked to age.[57] Younger women might also be preferred because they could give birth to healthier offspring with better survival chances.[58]

In studies of evolutionary psychology, youth is often associated with signs of health and vitality. Physical traits linked to youth – such as clear skin, physical fitness and energy – are subconscious indicators of good health and genetic quality. A recently published study from the Yale School of Medicine even showed that clear skin is generally associated with trustworthiness and intellect.[59]

Youthfulness is also linked to adaptability, learning potential and the ability to change. These qualities can be particularly important when choosing a long-term partner.

The problem everyone faces in partner selection is this: we cannot be certain if this partner will be a good choice in the long run. We can't predict a person's future financial success, psychological resilience or ability to adapt to changing life circumstances. All these traits are crucial for long-term relationship success.

Because of this uncertainty, traits like clear skin, physical fitness, energy, youthful appearance, and more might have often been useful decision-making shortcuts. These preferences, deeply rooted in our evolutionary past, might still shape our choices in modern society, even if the direct link between these traits and long-term success doesn't necessarily exist anymore.

Why might it be useful to consider this?

Understanding why we are still obsessed with youth and beauty is crucial for several reasons:

- It offers a broader perspective on human behaviour beyond mere cultural or social explanations. Recognizing that our preferences are rooted in deep-seated evolutionary processes helps us to understand where they come from – and why they might not just be silly or irrational.
- This knowledge also promotes a more empathetic view of ourselves and others. Our attraction to youth and beauty isn't necessarily superficial or trivial. It might simply be part of our evolutionary heritage. This understanding can lead to a more nuanced view of human desires and motivations.

However, it's equally important to acknowledge the role of modern societal influences. Our current environment amplifies these natural inclinations, sometimes to unhealthy extremes. Understanding the evolutionary basis doesn't justify the obsession. Instead, it provides context for why these traits are important in the first place.

Don't get me wrong: I'm not saying that ageing is solely biological and that our perspective on ageing can be explained purely by evolutionary biology or evolutionary psychology. Absolutely, age and ageing are also social and cultural phenomena. But it's not just a social construct. The biological and evolutionary perspectives play a role, too. It's social, cultural and biological. It's all of it at once.

Ageing in Different Cultures

Social anthropologists have highlighted this interplay of biology, culture and society in numerous works. Jay Sokolovsky's research, for example, provides insightful examples.[60] It shows how different cultures perceive and treat their elders, ranging from reverence and respect to marginalization and ageism.

In many Native American tribes, for instance, elders are revered as keepers of history and wisdom. They often serve as council members and are central to passing traditions down to younger generations.

In rural Japanese communities, older people are respected for their life experiences. They often play a significant role in community events and decision-making processes and are treated with a sort of 'childlike reverence.'

In cultures like the Maasai in Kenya and Tanzania, elders are an integral part of the social structure. They hold positions of authority within the community, oversee rituals, resolve disputes and guide the younger members.

Margaret Lock's work on menopause in Japan is also highly relevant in understanding cultural variations in the perception and experience of ageing.[61] In a Western context, the physical symptoms of menopause are emphasized – hot flashes, night sweats, osteoporosis. These symptoms are often highlighted both in medical literature and in the media, creating a narrative that menopause is a time of physical strain, something often treated with hormone replacement therapy, for instance. Lock shows that menopause in Western societies is also often associated with psychological and emotional challenges like depression, anxiety and a sense of loss. This view can be linked to broader societal attitudes toward ageing, where the focus is on decline and loss of youth.

This stands in stark contrast to Japan. Lock observed that Japanese women reported fewer and less severe menopausal symptoms than women in North America. She examined how societal attitudes, diet, lifestyle and cultural beliefs about ageing and femininity influenced these experiences. For example, in Japan, menopause wasn't heavily medicalized or viewed as a disorder. Instead, it was often recognized as a significant milestone of midlife. In many traditional three-generation households, the 50s are viewed as the prime of one's life, a period when individuals are at the height of their responsibilities.

This research highlights that the experience of menopause and, by extension, ageing, is not just a biological process. Ageing is deeply rooted in cultural contexts. It challenges the notion of a universal experience of physiological processes and underscores the importance of understanding ageing from a holistic perspective.

Recognizing that ageing is not only a biological inevitability but also a social and cultural construct is liberating for several reasons. First, it allows us to see ageing as a diverse and multifaceted experience.

It's not a uniform process defined solely by physical changes. This understanding opens up the possibility for a variety of ageing experiences influenced by cultural norms, beliefs and attitudes.

Second, understanding the cultural dimensions of ageing empowers us to challenge and potentially change negative stereotypes and practices. If our perceptions of ageing are not fixed but culturally shaped, then they can be reshaped. Societies can move away from narratives focused solely on decline and loss. Instead, they can adopt those that value the experience, wisdom and ongoing contributions of older people.

All this is especially important to consider when we seek to find better ways to deal with age and ageing in the context of a 100-year life.

AGEING IN THE 100-YEAR LIFE CYCLE

In the 100-year life, the focus isn't on eternal youth. In such a long life, physical changes like wrinkles and grey hair are inevitable. Our skin loses elasticity over time, hair can thin (or fall out entirely), and our physical strength might diminish. We might slow down and find that tasks which were once effortless now require more time and energy.

But this doesn't mean our lives, at a certain point, are just about decline. In a 100-year life, it's particularly valuable to view life as a 'life arc.' This perspective comes from Anne Karpf,[62] a renowned sociologist. In her concept of the life arc, Karpf emphasizes that every stage of life – childhood, youth, adulthood and old age as well as all the varying degrees of this in between – offers its own unique and valuable experiences and lessons. We shouldn't see ageing as a process of decline. Instead, we should see it as a journey through distinct phases – childhood, adolescence, parenthood, career one, career two and so on – each with its own purpose, challenges and opportunities to find meaning, grow, and contribute in new ways

Karpf suggests that a deeper understanding and appreciation of ageing and the ageing process allow us to see our life as a whole. This includes accepting that every age has its meaning and beauty, and that later life is a continuation of the journey, not its end. Through this lens, ageing becomes an integral and enriching part of human existence, not a process to be feared or avoided.

The life arc perspective can be applied in daily life in various ways, especially when dealing with age-related challenges. Here are some examples of how to practically apply this perspective.

- Instead of seeing your 40th birthday (or any milestone birthday) as a sign of decline, see it as a prompt to review what matters most to you now. Consider what you want to keep, what you're ready to let go of and what new ambitions might be taking shape.
- If you experience changes in your energy levels or physical abilities, see them not as setbacks but as invitations to recalibrate. You might build more rest into your week, adjust how you exercise or become more selective with how you spend your time and attention. When you see life as an arc, you come to expect these shifts in rhythm and recognize that needing more rest is not a failure but part of the shape of a well-lived life.
- If you spot more grey hair, hear from the doctor that you need multi-focal glasses or notice your knees complaining more after a long walk, take it as a nudge to check in with yourself. What do you need now? What's shifting? And how can you adapt with care rather than self-criticism? Ask yourself what you're glad to have experienced 20 years ago but wouldn't necessarily want to go through again, and let that be part of how you honour the phase you're in now.

In short, every stage of ageing can be an actively enriching time of growth if we acknowledge it as an inevitable part of the human condition.

Helmut Luft, a renowned researcher on ageing who shares Anne Karpf's view on the richness of each life stage, shared his insights shortly after celebrating his 100th birthday in an interview with a German daily newspaper.[63] In his view, it's not even about reaching a certain age in the first place. Rather, what matters is how to stay calm. How to remain friendly. How to participate in life even in old age without feeling despondent or resentful. Ageing, Luft says, isn't merely about physical fitness or appearance. It's an *Aufwärtsspirale* – an upward spiral – where you revisit familiar themes throughout life but perceive them with fresh, evolved perspectives each time.

Reframing Perceptions of Time

A clock is more than just a device; it symbolizes how we perceive time. It ticks relentlessly, minute by minute, hour by hour. This constant forward march of time shapes our view of the world. We often think chronologically: what happened yesterday is past, what comes tomorrow is the future. We place events on a linear timeline, with each moment being unique and then disappearing into the past.

In a 100-year life, the chronological perspective can be helpful. It allows us to see life in phases, each with its own significance and challenges. Chronology helps us organize and understand our life story. We recognize how past experiences influence future ones. Awareness of the passage of time can motivate us to pursue our long-term goals and appreciate the precious nature of each life stage.

But time doesn't have to be viewed only linearly. We can also see it cyclically. Nature shows us how to do this. Every year, spring returns, bringing with it blossoms and the awakening of nature. Every year, we celebrate birthdays, commemorate special events. Christmas, New Year's, annual traditions and festivals come around again and again. In a cyclical view of time, each event is part of a recurring cycle. It reminds us that life consists of recurring patterns and rhythms.

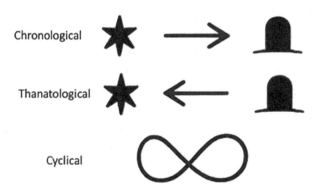

Cyclical thinking can also be valuable in a 100-year life, where we want to view life as an arc. Cyclical thinking emphasizes the renewal and recurrence of life events. In a long life, we experience many such cycles. They offer opportunities for new beginnings. Cycles remind us that after each phase of life, a new chance for renewal and growth awaits. Cyclical patterns provide a sense of consistency and security in a rapidly changing world. They create a connection between generations and offer a framework that endures over the years.

For a 100-year life, it's also valuable to view time thanatologically – that is, to think from the end. 'Thinking from the end' isn't something we do often, but sometimes it's part of our decision-making. For example, when buying a used car or bicycle, we would consider how long the vehicle will last and what it will cost us until the end of its usable life. We think about how the value of the car or bike will depreciate over time and how this will affect our investment. We ask ourselves how much benefit and joy it will bring us in its remaining years. So we calculate the price not just based on its current condition but also considering the potential endpoint of its use.

This type of thinking can also be applied to a 100-year life. By viewing our life from the end, we are encouraged to consider the long-term value of our decisions, activities and relationships. It helps us prioritize and make choices that bring us not only immediate fulfilment but also long-term satisfaction. Here are some examples.

- If we consider going (back) to university at an older age, we might imagine looking back at the end of our life: will we be grateful for the knowledge and experiences that further education has brought us?
- When contemplating starting a new relationship at 60, we might ask: will we feel enriched by the years spent with this person when we look back at the end of our life?
- In deciding whether to expand our home, we might think from our later years: will we look back on these changes as a source of joy and comfort that justified the investment?
- When considering a job change later in our career, we can ask: will we look back on this change as a positive influence on our final years?

In all these cases, the thanatological approach allows us to see our lives in the context of their finiteness and to make decisions based on long-term satisfaction and fulfilment. The thanatological perspective, where we view our lives from the end, can help us see present issues more calmly:

- When thinking about a difficult colleague, we can ask ourselves: will this be significant at the end of our life? In hindsight, it will likely appear as one of many encounters that had little impact on the overall course of our life.
- Similarly, with a micromanaging boss: in the context of an entire life, this experience will be just a small part of a much larger picture. In the end, what will matter more is how we responded to such challenges and what we learned from them.
- Even a bad year at work takes on a different perspective. Looking back on our life, such phases will likely be seen as moments of learning and growth, not permanent setbacks.
- In financial matters, like a poor stock market investment record, the end of our life can serve as a benchmark. In retrospect, long-term financial planning is likely to be more important than short-term fluctuations.

In short, this perspective helps us set priorities and live more consciously. By imagining how we want to look back on our life, we can make decisions that align with our true values and goals.

SIGNPOST

You're wandering through a historic old town in Southern Europe – maybe in Italy or Spain. You're enchanted by the charm of your surroundings, noticing the shuttered windows, so typical of this region: closed during the day to shield the homes from the scorching midday sun, and only opened in the evening to let in the cool evening air. Your gaze falls on the flowers cascading from balconies and windows, turning the streets into a colourful sea of blooms. Everything feels picturesque and relaxed. Traditional yet vibrant.

As you continue to stroll through the streets, you observe the people. Under the large sun umbrellas of the cafes, young and old sit together. The air is filled with laughter and cheerful chatter. Some elderly gentlemen are playing cards. Next to them, a group of young people are having a lively debate. Perhaps they're discussing the latest trends or their future plans?

What do you miss the most about the traditional three-stage life (education, work, retirement)?

- The predictability and structure of the career path?
- The clear goal of retirement as a reward for years of work?
- The single, intensive education phase in youth?
- The clear expectations for each life stage?

What aspects of the multistage life worry you the most?

- The uncertainty and necessity of constant change?
- The pressure to keep learning and developing throughout life?
- The challenge of balancing multiple careers and life phases?
- The potential financial instability from frequent changes?

Which aspects of the three-stage model do you not miss?

- The narrow, conservative ideas of how a life should be 'properly' led?
- The rigid role expectations dictating what is appropriate at a certain age?
- The outdated and rigid concepts of success and life planning?
- The assumption that relaxation begins only at retirement?

What do you see as the greatest benefits of a multistage life?

- The variety of career opportunities and life experiences?
- The flexibility to adapt life to personal needs?
- The possibility to plan your life yourself?
- The ability to better balance work and leisure throughout life?

Now, you flip through old photo albums and look at a picture of yourself as a five-year-old playing in the sandbox around the corner. Other children are around you, but you can't recall their names today. A class photo from fourth grade catches your attention. What was the teacher's name? Your eyes scan the faces, some familiar, some now strange.

Then you come across photos of your first love. A picture of the two of you being silly together makes you smile – how strange and exciting it was back then. You notice that you had your quirks even then. At 21, as you see in a photo, you pulled your feet up in a specific way while reading on the sofa, a habit you still have today.

Another picture shows you at 30 on a beach, laughing exuberantly. But you remember it as a time full of personal insecurities, despite the apparent happiness in the photo. These pictures make you reflect.

1. Go online and search for the 'Death Clock.' Find out how many days you have left, statistically speaking. Now imagine you receive £2 million – an unexpected inheritance. That's enough money to meet your needs now and until your last day. How would you live your life from now on? What would you do with the money? Would you change anything? Let yourself go. Don't hold back your dreams. Describe a life that is complete, that is entirely yours.

2. Imagine you still have the £2 million. You visit your doctor, who tells you that you have five to ten years left to live. The good news is you will never feel ill again. The bad news is you won't know the exact time of your death. What will you do with the time you have left? Will you change your life, and how will you do it?

3. This time, your doctor shocks you with the news that you have only one day left to live. Pay attention to the feelings that arise when confronted with your mortality. Ask yourself: which dreams will remain unfulfilled? What do you wish you had achieved or become? What would you have liked to do? Did you miss out on something?

These questions are inspired by George Kinder's "three questions for life planning."[64]

We're wrapping up Part 2.

In this section, we've tried to understand why planning for a 100-year life is tricky.

We've discovered that managing money is tough because our evolutionary behaviours and psychological tendencies often clash with the demands of modern financial planning.

Instincts that were once vital for survival can mislead us in the complex world of finances. Moreover, the challenges of managing and saving money are partly due to an evolutionary formed makeup that promotes instant gratification and undervalues long-term thinking.

We've seen that retirement planning, in particular, is a mental challenge. It's not just because we seek and prioritize immediate satisfaction but also because, over the last 150 years, we've formed expectations that no longer match the cultural, social and economic spirit of the times. This is a huge mental hurdle.

Finally, we accept that longevity itself is challenging because we were never prepared to live this long. We face the task of adapting our life plans, healthcare and social structures to accommodate a longer lifespan. The idea of a life that could span a century requires rethinking work, retirement, personal development, relationships and how we think about age and ageing itself. This, too, is mentally taxing.

The combination of all these aspects helps us understand that it's not our fault that we find it difficult to fund a happy, long life. We're not stupid, bad or irrational. It's the historical context in which we live that creates these challenges. Our current struggles with planning for a long life reflect the fact that our societies, institutions and personal expectations are still adapting to the reality of unprecedented longevity. This understanding allows us to view our own weaknesses with greater compassion and approach the design of our long lives with more understanding and creativity.

Can we move on? We've identified enough problems. It's time for solutions.

PART 3

Self-Knowledge:
The Key to
a Prosperous
100-year Life

In this final part, we look at how to make smarter financial life planning decisions. Now we're getting to the nitty-gritty. How do we achieve financial wellbeing? How do we earn, spend and manage our money in a way that makes us happy today, tomorrow and in the future? How do you find your path to prosperity?

The key to this ... drumroll, please ... is self-knowledge.

We need to learn to understand what makes us happy. Of course, we do! Without this knowledge, we can't earn, spend and manage our money in harmony with what makes us happy.

Additionally, we need to learn to recognize what prevents us from dealing with paying attention to what makes us happy in our daily lives. Because the problem, in a nutshell, is this: we live in a world full of distractions. It's not just family, work and daily obligations that demand our full attention. No, we're also surrounded by a number of clever mechanisms and systems that know how to get our attention. The often given and well-intended advice to "just ignore" things like Black Friday offers, stock market crashes or notifications received on our phones misses the point. How these systems work and their particularly strong effects on us is a part of self-knowledge.

Moreover, we need a strong connection to our future self. Specifically to the worries, desires and needs of our future self. We need to figure out what truly matters to us and where our priorities lie. How to achieve this will be revealed in the pages that follow.

Let's get started.

CHAPTER 6

FINDING HAPPINESS IN THE EVERYDAY: UNDERSTANDING WHAT MATTERS

For a long and happy life, we need one very important ingredient: the knowledge of what makes us happy. It's kind of obvious.

"The happy life." I realize that it may sound superficial or silly. A bit like naïve bliss. Maybe a bit like that famous song "Happy" by Pharrell Williams. Who needs a roof over their head, Williams suggests, when you know that happiness is the ultimate truth? What contributes more to a happy life than clapping along to an uplifting four-four beat?

Well, it's not that simple, of course. The word 'happiness' is under stress. And the many cautionary voices often have a point: first, there are those who urge us to distinguish between joy, happiness and contentment. While joy is often a fleeting, intense feeling that arises from specific moments or events, happiness refers to a more general state of wellbeing. Contentment, on the other hand, is a deeper, lasting sense of fulfilment and acceptance of life as it is.

Neuroscientists warn that the constant pursuit of happiness is not only unrealistic but also potentially harmful.[65] They say that our brains are not designed for a permanent state of happiness and that constantly chasing it can lead to psychological stress and dissatisfaction.[66] Many philosophers, including Aristotle, emphasize that a happy life requires more than just the feeling of happiness at all times. They suggest focusing on *flourishing*, a state that includes accepting and integrating failure, disappointment, sorrow and other negative emotions into a fulfilling life.[67]

When I speak of a 'happy life,' I refer to the concept of happiness as developed by Paul Dolan, a behavioural scientist at the London School of Economics. He argues that a happy life encompasses both experiences of pleasure and a sense of purpose.[68]

He writes in his book, *Happiness by Design*, that *pleasure* arises from experiences and activities that make us feel good, such as enjoying a delicious meal, having a heartfelt conversation with a friend, or relaxing in a peaceful environment. These experiences generate positive emotions and sensations. Pleasure is usually experienced in the present, but the anticipation of future happy moments (like an upcoming holiday) can contribute to a long-term sense of happiness. Similarly, memories of beautiful experiences (like a concert a few years ago) can offer lasting joy and positively impact our wellbeing.[69]

Purpose, on the other hand, is characterized by a sense of meaningful engagement and contribution. Purpose gives our actions and experiences significance and depth by involving ourselves in activities that contribute to something beyond ourselves. These can be modest things – like attending a parents' evening.

Purpose is something we feel here and now, but it also extends into the long-term future by providing a sense of direction and contributing to what matters to us. This involves engaging in activities and goals that make us feel useful, competent or valuable. This could include working on a challenging project, volunteering for a cause we care about, raising children or pursuing personal goals that require effort and dedication.

According to Dolan, a happy life isn't just about pleasant moments. And it doesn't just consist of purposeful moments, either. We can lead a happy life that feels equally pleasant and meaningful when pleasure and purpose are in balance. This balance ensures that we not only enjoy the pleasures of the present but also invest in activities that promise deeper satisfaction and contribute to our sense of identity and worth in the long term.

A 'happy life' often sounds a bit Californian in many self-help books: fabulous trips, jet skiing, yoga on the beach or sipping home-made cocktails in infinity pools. But you can achieve the same – or even a higher – level of happiness if you've discovered that a pizza with the family, long walks along the canal or a quiet morning with a good book gives you a sense of contentment or relaxation.

The same applies to purpose: we all know the high-flyers who advise us to find our purpose, define our vision and plan our weeks, months and years in line with this vision. But the feeling of being useful, competent or valuable can also be found in smaller things and more mundane activities: planning the next family holiday, starting a herb garden or helping your child find the right pieces for their next architectural Lego masterpiece. Or by baking the perfect sourdough loaf or organizing a community clean-up event.

The advice to "find your purpose!" can feel daunting. "There's a lot of purpose-anxiety out there," says Jordan Grumet in an interview with Christine Benz.[70] But "your purpose" doesn't have to be any change-the-world-for-the-better massive type of thing. It can be whatever little contribution that makes you feel useful or competent.

Take a moment to think:
- When were you truly happy in the last five years? What about last month? Last week? And today or yesterday?
- When did you feel truly useful in the last five years? What about last month? Last week? And today or yesterday?

ONE-HUNDRED-YEAR
LIFE HAPPINESS

One-hundred-year life happiness means making decisions that bring not only short-term joy but also contribute to long-term happiness. An example of this is choosing a career that, while challenging, promotes personal growth and fulfilment in the long run.

By focusing on 100-year life happiness, we can better navigate the many phases of our longer, healthier lives. We can make adjustments that enhance our long-term wellbeing. This ensures that our life remains pleasant and meaningful, not just in our younger years, but also as we age, when our needs and desires change.

100-YEAR LIFE HAPPINESS IS BALANCED GRATIFICATION

Over the course of a long life, we must learn to find the right balance between immediate and delayed gratification.

Instant gratification is easy to recognize. We experience it when we enjoy a fast-food meal, satisfying our immediate need for food. However, in the long run, it may be unhealthy. Homer Simpson is perhaps the poster child for instant gratification. In a classic moment, his wife Marge tells him, "One day, these kids will move out, and you'll regret not spending more time with them." Homer grabs a bottle of vodka and replies, "That's a problem for future Homer. Man, I don't envy that guy."

Delayed gratification, on the other hand, is seen when decisions are being made to positively affect the outcomes for the future self – perhaps at expense of the present self. This includes regularly saving for the long-term (including retirement). It also includes pursuing long-term educational goals that require time and commitment today for the prospect of a fulfilling career later on. Or building deep relationships, which require patience and understanding but result in lasting friendships and partnerships.

The challenge lies in finding the balanced path. One that neither prioritizes only immediate nor only delayed gratification. It's about *balanced gratification*. Balanced gratification allows us to enjoy the small pleasures of everyday life while not losing sight of long-term goals and values.

Maybe there are fewer immediate bursts of joy. And fewer expectations that 'one day' everything will be perfect. Instead, there are more modest but balanced moments of satisfaction spread over longer periods.[71]

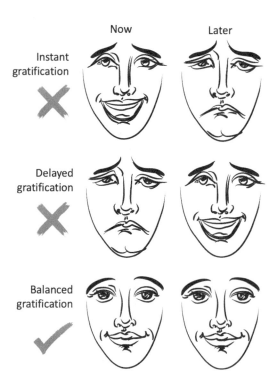

The concept of balanced gratification can also be applied to understanding pain. Immediate pain can be burdensome in the short term. However, it can often lead to personal growth and a better quality of life in the long term. An example of this is a divorce. It can bring immediate emotional pain and uncertainty. But in the long run, it can lead to a more fulfilling life. Suppressing conflicts in relationships may seem more comfortable in the short term. It leads to short-term peace but also carries the risk of bigger problems later on. Long-term, deferred pain can lead to deeper emotional upheaval and problems.

Facing a burnout might require taking a career break. But in the long run, with time and perspective, we find explanations for what happened and move on. And this offers a chance to reassess life priorities and live healthier into old age. Avoiding regular health check-ups provides more comfort in the here and now. But it can pose serious health risks in the long run.

Ignoring financial problems avoids short-term stress. But it likely leads to long-term financial difficulties. Quitting an unsatisfactory job might cause short-term financial insecurity. But in the long run, it could pave the way for a more fulfilling career.

Here, too, the concept of balanced gratification applies. It teaches us to accept the challenges of the moment while planning for the future. This way, we create a life that is fulfilling and meaningful both in the present and in the long run.

To achieve this balance, it is worth considering the previously mentioned time perspectives: the chronological, the cyclical and the thanatological view. Or in other words: forward, steady and backward.

- The chronological perspective views life from now into the future: forward. It helps us make decisions that consider both our current needs and our long-term goals. In this perspective, we ask ourselves questions like:
  "What steps can I take today to achieve my future goals?"
  "How do my decisions today impact my long-term plans?"
  "What skills and resources should I develop now to be successful in the future?"

- The cyclical perspective considers what has always brought us joy or pain. Christmas holidays, monthly bills, school events, summer vacations, weddings, meetings with friends – the recurring events. In this perspective, we ask ourselves questions like:
  "How do I experience this?"
  "What about it brings me joy?"
  "What makes me feel competent, useful or valuable?"
  "What do I not like about it?"
  "What would I like to do differently next time and why?"
  "What about it causes me stress?"

- The thanatological perspective looks back from the end of life to the here and now: backward. It helps us recognize which decisions are truly important and encourages us to choose paths that lead to a fulfilling and meaningful life. In this view, we ask ourselves:
  "Will this decision seem important to me at the end of my life?"
  "What memories do I want to create and leave behind?"
  "What values and principles do I want to prioritize in my life to be at peace with myself in the end?"

These three perspectives enable us to create a life that is fulfilling and meaningful both in the present and in the long term. They help us find the right balance between immediate and delayed gratification. And they aid in managing both the immediate and delayed pain in our lives.

AVOIDING HAPPINESS TRAPS

Here, I'll uncover two traps we often fall into in everyday life that prevent us from finding long-term happiness.

The Justification Trap

Maybe you're unhappy in your job because your boss is an overbearing micromanager. But you keep convincing yourself that it's a good job because the company is prestigious.

Or perhaps you're unhappy in your relationship because your partner treats you poorly. Yet you tell yourself, "I love him," justifying why you stay in the relationship. The dissatisfaction you feel is the *experience*; the justification, "I love him," is the *evaluation*.

Two more examples: maybe you feel uncomfortable at large family gatherings, but you tell yourself it's important to be there because "family is family."

Or perhaps you have a hobby that frustrates you because you see no progress. However, you convince yourself that it's good for you because it's 'creative.'

You see, there's a difference between what you *experience* (the overbearing boss, the poorly-behaved partner, the annoying family gatherings or the frustrating hobby) and how you *evaluate* the situation. It's another key insight from Paul Dolan.

A simple rule of thumb to uncover whether it's an experience or an evaluation is: "Do I feel it? Or do I justify it?"

If your immediate emotional reaction to a situation is negative – like stress, frustration or dissatisfaction – then that's your actual experience. However, if you find yourself coming up with reasons the situation is still good or right despite how it feels, then it's an evaluation. This rule helps distinguish genuine feelings from subsequent justifications or rationalizations.

The Availability Trap

When we think about what brings us pleasure and purpose in life, we tend to focus on what comes to mind first. After a lovely garden party, we might think that spending time with family is most important. After a great concert, we might feel that music is indispensable. Or after a successful project at work, we might think we want to work forever.

The problem: by focusing on individual things that bring us pleasure and purpose, we often overlook what is generally known to contribute to long-term happiness and wellbeing. We concentrate too much on what is immediately available to us. We then forget what is broadly known to be contributing to life happiness.

THE MASTER LIST OF THINGS
THAT MAKE US HAPPY

Let's take a look at a master list of things that, according to psychology, neuroscience and behavioural science, are known to be extremely important components of long-term wellbeing:

- Strong, positive relationships with family, friends and community are generally crucial. Social support and (the feeling of) being connected to others are linked to higher levels of happiness in numerous studies.
- Regular physical activity, a healthy diet and sufficient sleep are fundamental for good mental health and happiness. Exercise is known to reduce symptoms of depression and anxiety.
- Stress management, resilience and support for mental health issues are important. Practices like mindfulness and gratitude can improve emotional wellbeing.
- Pursuing goals, especially those that are challenging yet achievable, and developing skills in various areas of life can create a sense of fulfilment and satisfaction.
- Having control over one's own life and making decisions that align with personal values and interests is important for happiness. This includes the feeling that one's actions are self-determined and voluntary.[72]
- Experiencing positive emotions such as joy, awe, contentment and love contributes to happiness. This can be fostered through activities that bring pleasure and satisfaction.
- In the wealthiest countries, there are strong positive correlations between green spaces and happiness. This suggests that green spaces play a significant role in increasing happiness and reducing loneliness.[73]
- A positive attitude and the ability to see opportunities in challenges are linked to higher levels of happiness. This doesn't mean ignoring problems, but rather approaching life with a hopeful and constructive mindset.

We need introspection – looking inward to recognize and evaluate what we experience and how we behave. It's essential.

But introspection alone is not enough. Our System 1 can sometimes lead us astray, such as through the availability trap. We tend to focus on what immediately comes to mind and often overlook what contributes to our happiness in the long run. That's why it's important to also incorporate scientifically backed insights into our considerations.

A study we conducted at the Centre for Behavioural Research found that about half of those surveyed had a financial plan, often including aspects like retirement savings and building reserves. Many also considered what brought them pleasure and purpose in life. Interestingly though, when these individuals were presented with the master list above, 75% stated that they could also incorporate elements from this comprehensive list into their financial plan – things they had previously overlooked.

These findings suggest that a combination of personal introspection and scientifically backed knowledge can lead to more effective and satisfying decisions, both in the financial realm and life in general. Your path to prosperity likely consolidates *your personal needs* and desires with what *objectively contributes* to long-term happiness and wellbeing. This is how we can create a more balanced and fulfilling life.

HAPPINESS IN SPENDING AND EARNING MONEY

In the 100-year life, we strive for balanced satisfaction, not just the happy life in the here and now, and not just the happy life in the future. We aim for a happy life today and in the future. Or vice versa: in the future and today.

How can this be applied to how we should spend money?

Often, we are tempted to jump on great deals. The Black Friday season is one such time of year when our instincts and emotions are lured into making quick purchases.

Who knows if it's really a good deal? The seller? Or you?

The correct answer, of course, is: only you should know.

The longer answer is: only you know, but only if you understand what brings you pleasure and purpose.

A 20% discount on a Sony PlayStation can be a good deal if gaming is a source of joy for us or if it allows us to spend quality time with family. Here, the purchase becomes an investment in pleasure and purpose.

A 30% discount on a designer perfume might seem attractive. But it's only a good deal if the perfume truly suits our personality or gives us a sense of satisfaction that lasts beyond the moment of purchase.

A smartwatch at a 50% discount depends on whether this technology makes our daily life easier. It might even promote our health by encouraging us to be more active.

The point is, it depends!

The true value of a deal is not just in seasonal bargains but in all spending. An expensive city-centre apartment is worthwhile if the quality of life and the short commutes bring us daily time and joy. A larger car makes sense if circumstances require it and it adds value to our lives. But often, a bicycle or public transport suffices. A holiday in Vietnam is a wonderful experience as long as it adds joy or meaning to our life and isn't just about status. A holiday in the Cotswolds could be just as enriching if it meets our needs for relaxation and nature experiences.

Have you heard of the millionaire formula? It preaches delaying today's pleasures in favour of future wealth. For example, a daily cappuccino is wasted money according to the millionaire formula. If we saved that money, we could set aside a certain amount over ten years and, through the power of compound interest, it would grow to an impressive sum. Yes, that's mathematically correct. But perhaps the money spent on the cappuccino isn't wasted. Maybe it's a small ritual of self-care that brightens the day. Perhaps it satisfies a need for connection and belonging, mindfulness and presence, or community and identity.

As I said, it depends. And I don't know the answer. Only you (can) know.

When my twins were seven years old, we made the decision to take a two-month summer break during their school holidays. We interrailed through Europe, experienced a few different countries and cultures – had a thrill crossing borders. To make it happen, we took parental leave, which meant forgoing our regular income and allocating a significant portion of our savings to cover the expenses. The millionaires' formula would have questioned whether this was a prudent choice. If we had chosen to continue earning an income and invested the surplus money in a long-term savings plan, the power of compound interest might have allowed our savings to grow to a very substantial amount over the course of 30 years. Was that decision foolish? The answer isn't straightforward: it depends. While financially we might have secured a more robust future, the experiences and the joy we shared as a family during that summer are equally, and to us more, valuable. Balancing present happiness with future security is a complex equation. I'm not telling you that this is the way to do it, but for us it was one way, considering what we felt might be important to us now and in the future.[74]

Self-knowledge is the key to the right spending behaviour: it helps us choose expenditures that enhance our current quality of life without compromising the future. It teaches us to invest in experiences and objects that enrich our sense of meaning. It allows us to think about now, but also beyond the moment and invest in things that bring lasting satisfaction.

Spending money is one side of the coin.

Earning money is the other side of the same coin.

For a successful 100-year life, it's unsustainable to stay in a job that doesn't, over time, give you a good balance of pleasure and purpose. An unsatisfying job likely contributes to lower life satisfaction, reduced productivity and impaired relationships. It will, over the long term, likely have financial implications.

That's why it pays off – again, over the long term – to reflect whether the way we earn money makes us happy. And whether the job is a good fit for other variables that matter – like health, family, leisure time and personal wellbeing.

Many appear to be doing this: in the UK, the number of adults over the age of 25 who're taking part in education and reeducation programmes (often online course offered by a university) has risen constantly over recent decades.[75] It suggests that many people are not just changing employers, but careers, too.

How, though, may we work out what other ways of earning money may be more appealing?

It may be worth exploring different career paths by a variety of professions and industries – for instance, through old school or university acquaintances or former colleagues who have taken different paths. Engaging with other ways to earn a living can help us understand what kind of work we enjoy. You might want to create an archive of job profiles and careers that also seem interesting to you. You can include jobs you've come across in your network, read about in articles, biographies and job descriptions, and keep this collection up to date.

When exploring, consider which aspects of a profession are particularly appealing. This could be the nature of the daily tasks, the values of the profession or the type of challenges typical for that career. It can be beneficial to talk to people already working in the fields that interest you. LinkedIn is excellent for this (I find that, anyway). But there are, of course, other alternatives. Either way, such conversations offer insights into the daily realities of different professions and can reveal whether the reality matches your expectations.

If feasible (for example, with funds from a transition fund), you could gain practical experience in various fields through internships, volunteering or projects. Traditionally, internships occur during the first phase of life (the education phase). In a 100-year life, this need not be the case (employers are increasingly adapting). Why not do an internship at a radio station at 50 if a radio career seems like the next step?

If you find yourself needing a hot bath every Friday night to recover from work, or if you can hardly wait for the next summer holiday even though it's not yet November, this indicates a work life that is neither pleasant nor meaningful. Your job shouldn't cause misery over the long term. A suitable job leverages your skills, talents and interests. And it should be a good match considering your circumstances. It's important to recognize that as our personal and social contexts evolve over time, so too should our approach to how we earn a living.

Recognizing and Questioning Expectations

In all of this, it's important to consider the role of expectations. In our quest for pleasure and purpose in our work, seeking a career that not only pays but also provides fulfilment is undoubtedly challenging. Historically, this is a new expectation. One hundred and fifty years ago, no one would have aimed to find a job that makes them happy. That would have been a ridiculous goal. But we must also recognize that perfect satisfaction in every area of life – be it work, family or relationships – is more of an ideal than a constant reality. This insight doesn't diminish our pursuit but rather enriches it with a layer of pragmatism.

"The trajectory of a happy life is shaped by expectations," says author and behavioural finance expert Brian Portnoy.[76] This means that the core of our satisfaction not only depends on experiencing pleasure and purpose but also on the expectations we hold. It is commendable to strive for work that makes us happy. But it's equally important to realize that no role is without difficulties and problems. The world of work, like life itself, is full of imperfections and unpredictable challenges. Accepting this tempers our ambitions with realism and prevents us from falling into disillusionment when our hopes inevitably clash with reality.

Remember Donald Winnicott's two aspects of the self? (We discussed this in connection with the stories of my friends Anna and Simona.) The true self reflects our deepest desires and strives for work that genuinely fulfils us and aligns with our values. The false self, on the other hand, chases success as defined by others, which can hinder our true happiness. By understanding these two sides, we can better decide what we really want. We learn to set realistic goals and not be guided by unattainable ideals. This way, we find a path that suits our true self and brings genuine satisfaction.

Therefore, as we strive to weave pleasure and purpose into our careers, the wisdom of managing our expectations is very helpful. It's a balancing act of aiming high enough to stay motivated while being grounded enough to accept life's inherent imperfections. By adopting this approach, we cannot only seek happiness in our work but also cultivate deep and lasting satisfaction in our 100-year life.

STAYING FOCUSED IN A WORLD
FULL OF DISTRACTIONS

You probably know Facebook. And you might know that Facebook started as a social network for Harvard University students. Initially, the network's sole aim was to connect people. Mark Zuckerberg launched the website in 2004 from his dorm room. The platform quickly spread from Harvard to other universities and eventually became accessible to everyone. From the simple idea of creating a social network for students, Facebook grew into a global company. Today, it has billions of users and is far removed from its humble beginnings.

Facebook quickly became keen on getting more users. Not just that, Facebook wanted users to spend a lot of time on the platform. After all, their attention is exactly what Facebook (and other social media platforms) sells to its advertisers. Did you know that?

To capture user attention, a lot of experimenting was done. And with the results from such studies, some of the more modest initial visions were abandoned.

The notification symbol – at the top of the blue bar – is a good example. Initially, Facebook designers preferred a blue symbol. It matched Facebook's style and was considered "subtle and harmless." There was a problem, though: messages that could have kept users engaged on the platform were being ignored. Facebook designers pondered what to do. They experimented and tested assumptions. Then, one day, they found a solution: changing the notification symbol from blue to red. And suddenly – boom – usage increased dramatically.[77] Today, you see the red notification symbol everywhere. Missed call? The red dot on the app icon alerts you. New message in WhatsApp? The red dot forces itself on you. An update from a colleague on LinkedIn? Hard to miss with the red dot at the top of the bar. And so on.

Why the red dot everywhere? It's simple: the design choice is based on psychological principles. Red is a colour that naturally grabs human attention. The colour red is often associated with alarm and urgency. That's why red is frequently used for stop signs, emergency vehicles and warning lights. In the context of Facebook and other platforms, the red notification symbol leverages these innate reactions to red to capture user attention. The aim is to make notifications more notice-able and thereby increase user interaction with the platform.

All this is part of a broader field of research known as 'colour psy-chology.' This field explores how different colours influence human behaviour and decision-making. The point is this: big companies like Facebook know something about you – how you function, how to get your attention and how your behaviour can be influenced – that you probably don't know. By engaging you in things like this, they prevent you from doing other important things. Things like self-reflection or letting your mind wander. Or allowing thoughts that are also present but do not surface due to constant distraction.

"DO I REALLY NEED THIS?"

Knowledge about how instincts, emotions and habit formation work is not only widespread among big tech companies like Face-book but also among many retailers and online shops. It's crucial to understand that we live in an environment that often hinders better financial conduct.

We all know it's important to avoid excessive debt. But, often, we're tempted to pay with a credit card at the end of the month when money is tight, and that shirt would be perfect for a party. We know it's important to build savings. But we often spend our money on subscriptions we haven't questioned in a long time. Spotify, Netflix, the gym, magazines, meal boxes, designer coffee – do you really need all that? Perhaps you do. But only you know. Maybe they're just little financial gremlins you forgot about?

Another example in this context is services like Amazon Prime, whose free delivery has significantly increased impulse purchases.[78] Buying without much thought is triggered by many websites through manipulative practices: EU researchers recently found that 97% of websites use such methods, from fake countdown timers ("Last chance, limited-time offer prices") to pressure sales techniques ("Only £30 more for free shipping on orders over £100").[79]

These practices are not only ubiquitous but also evolving rapidly and becoming more sophisticated.

An increasing concern for many is the so-called hypernudging. This is a proactive and dynamic system of influence strategies. It uses methods to subtly steer user behaviour. Through advanced metrics and simpler tracking methods, organizations can now capture and analyse individual data in real time. This allows them to personalize user experiences in ways that promote specific behavioural changes. The use of A/B testing enhances the ability of organizations to experiment with different strategies and identify the most effective methods to influence user behaviour.[80]

What can we do? We can't wait for national or international regulators to pass laws. By the time laws are implemented, the industry has already evolved. And to complicate matters: many of these practices operate in a grey area between legitimate persuasion and illegitimate manipulation.

What we need is self-knowledge about how these things affect us.

———————————

Recognizing and Responding to Manipulative Sales Practices
- Time-limited offers create a sense of urgency and can lead to hasty decisions. The next time you encounter a time-limited offer, remind yourself that this urgency is often artificially created. They're trying to rush you into a purchase.
- Social proof, like customer reviews, strongly influences our buying decisions. Approach such reviews with scepticism. Ask yourself if they should genuinely affect your decision or if they're just a sales tactic.
- Showing an originally higher price makes a reduced price seem more attractive. Remember, the original price might have been inflated to make the discounted price look better.
- Free offers or bonuses give the impression of a better deal. Consider if the main purchase would still be appealing without the free offer.
- Product placement can influence our buying behaviour (e.g. pricier items at eye level). Be aware of product positioning and ask yourself if your interest in a product is influenced by its placement.
- "Only a few left in stock" messages create a sense of scarcity and encourage purchases. Question whether the item is genuinely scarce or if it's just a sales strategy.

- Easy and quick payment options can lead to less considered purchases. Take your time to think about your purchase. Don't be swayed
  by the convenience of fast payment.
- "Customers who bought this also bought ..." suggests you're missing
  out if you don't follow suit. Be aware that this is a sales tactic and might
  not align with your needs.
- Bundle offers suggest better value for money. Consider whether
  you really need all the components of the bundle or if they're unnecessary extras.

In general, to better understand and control the influence of all these
factors on our behaviour, it's helpful to consider the interplay of triggers, reactions and reflections. A trigger (like the red dot on Facebook)
catches our attention. It's specifically designed to provoke an immediate and often emotional response, a reaction intended to drive us
toward a particular behaviour or purchase decision.

The immediate reaction to a trigger is often intuitive and emotional. It ranges from excitement or a sense of urgency to the desire
to buy a product or use a service. These reactions are typically quick
and automatic, without us being aware of the underlying triggers or
considering the long-term consequences of our actions.

This is where the importance of reflection comes in. Through
reflection, we can better protect ourselves from manipulative sales
techniques and make decisions that truly serve our best interests.
Remember: it shouldn't be the sellers who determine whether something's good. You should know it! Sellers don't want you to think too
much. They want you to just get the thing.

"DO I REALLY NEED TO KNOW THIS?"

We know it already: news often focuses on negative events and
neglects positive developments. Yet, when a major political conflict
erupts in another country, we read about it in horror. When there's a
big scandal in local politics, we're immediately drawn to it and follow

every new development. And when a major stock market crash happens, we worry about our financial future.

News presents stories in a way that promotes a specific reaction: outrage, pity, disgust. These reactions may seem appropriate at first glance, but often we are subtly nudged to forget or ignore our own feelings and thoughts about these events.

Take, for example, the coverage of natural disasters. The media often focuses on the extent of the destruction and the suffering of those affected. This emphasis is understandable, but it can lead us to overlook the resilience and courage of people in these situations. Deep down, we may feel admiration and hope in the face of their strength and solidarity. But these feelings are rarely highlighted in the news.

Another example is the portrayal of political leaders. Media can make us despise or admire certain individuals based on a one-sided depiction of their actions and statements. In reality, we might have a more nuanced or even opposite view of these people, based on our own values and beliefs.

Finally, financial news shapes how we think about and handle money. Reports that American stocks have broken records over the past six months might tempt us to invest hastily. At the same time, experts' warnings about the weakness of government bonds might make us worry about our safe investments. And when influencers talk about a new rush on Bitcoin, we might feel tempted to dive into cryptocurrencies.

News can trigger strong emotions that affect our long-term financial plans. If we think everything is just speculation, we might avoid long-term investments altogether. Reports of quick profits can lead us to make risky decisions. Or if we're convinced that traditional investments are the safest, negative reports can cause panic.

One of the best investment strategies is the 'buy and hold' principle, where you set aside a certain amount of what you earn and invest it in your cost-efficient long-term savings plan without paying too much attention to short-term market movements to avoid the temptation to sell or switch strategies. Ronald Read, a janitor, amassed an incredible fortune of $8 million by the time he died in 2014.[81] He didn't inherit wealth. He didn't win the lottery. His secret to success was quite simple: he saved consistently and leveraged the power of compound interest. This story shows that, when it comes to money, it's often better to ignore daily news and stick to a simple decision.

The point is: we need self-knowledge. We must recognize the impact news has on us and how detrimental this impact can be to our long-term success. News can distract us from our own emotions, instincts, motivations, beliefs and values. It often shifts our attention to short-term events and trends, causing us to lose sight of the bigger, long-term picture – and a picture that's far more relevant to us and in our control. On your path to prosperity, you need to learn to question the news and focus on your own long-term goals and values.

Rather beautifully, in the English language, you say that you *pay* attention. In my native German, you'd say that you 'give attention' or 'direct attention.'

'Paying' attention highlights that attention is a scarce resource. We've got to be economical with it. I cannot play Monopoly with my kids and listen to music at the same time. I can't have a dinner conversation with my wife and answer WhatsApp messages at the same time.

To pay attention to one thing inevitably means not paying attention to something else.

I'm writing these lines in the build-up to the US election in November 2024. Many of us have been paying a lot of attention to what's happening over there. We read clever interpretations of what Trump climbing into a garbage truck in Green Bay, Wisconsin, may do to voters in the swing state of Pennsylvania. And we heard how appealing it may be to deprived voter groups to see Kamala Harris participating in a civil rights protest as a toddler.

Here's the thing: it's taking a lot of our bandwidth. And paying attention to what's happening in the US inevitably means we can't pay attention to something else.

More important news – that you don't read about in the news – may be this:

- Time to buy your partner a bunch of flowers.
- Take an hour to enjoy a quiet walk in nature.

- Organize a catchup with your best friend from high school days.
- Dedicate some time to a hobby or activity that brings you joy.
- Ask yourself when you last felt competent.

Ask yourself when reading headlines: why do I need to know this? How, if at all, does this affect my plans? What am I not reading in the news that may be more relevant to me – and in my control, too?[82]

"DO I NEED MY PHONE ALL THE TIME?"

Now, let's talk about something that's really close to your heart: your phone. How much time do you spend on your phone? How many seconds pass before you whip it out to escape boredom? For instance, when you're waiting for a train. Or standing in a queue. Or waiting for the kettle to boil. Usually, it doesn't take long – ten seconds, max: then the messages are checked, the WhatsApp status reviewed, social media scrolled and emails briefly skimmed.

There's increasing evidence that our brains need a break from constant information processing to be able to focus and be creative. Researchers have found that just the presence of a smartphone can reduce brain performance. In a 2023 study, the concentration ability of 800 smartphone users was measured while their phones were in plain sight, face down on a desk, in their pockets or in another room. The result? Even when the phones were silenced, the cognitive capacity of participants was significantly reduced if their phone was in view or easily accessible. Parts of their brains were too busy not looking at their phones.[83] This means that your smartphone could be affecting your ability to rest and recharge, even if it's just in your pocket or lying on the table next to you while you read this book.

The issues we've discussed before – the notification symbols, the techniques encouraging purchases, the distractions from the news – are all amplified by the phone. We are constantly 'hooked' – in the words of Nir Eyal, author of the book *Hooked: How to Build Habit-Forming Products*. The blurb of the German translation of the book says: "This book is essential for anyone who wants to create a product that their users can't put down and imagine life without."[84]

The English original praises that readers will get equipped "with practical insights to create user habits that stick; actionable steps for building products people love; and riveting examples, from the iPhone to Twitter, Instagram and Google."

At a conference in 2017, Eyal described how he protects himself from the very techniques he promotes. He has installed a timer in his house that shuts off the internet at the same time every day.

Is this the solution? Regularly locking away the phone or turning it off completely? Perhaps. Even in Silicon Valley, there are increasingly more private schools that ban phones and tablets for children.[85]

Tanya Goodin, an expert on digital detox and author of the book *My Brain Has Too Many Tabs Open*, explores the impact of this constant information flood. She says that one of the few remaining sacred places where most people don't take their phones is the shower. Maybe that's why you sometimes have sudden moments of clarity or good ideas while washing your hair.

I try to reduce my phone usage where I can. I used to listen to podcasts on my bike ride to work. Not anymore. It's about a 50-minute journey on cycle paths that used to be train tracks. Safe but boring; you only find other cyclists and pedestrians. I used to think it was the perfect route to listen to interesting podcasts. Nowadays, I keep the phone off and notice: after 20 minutes of cycling through the emptiness, funny, new and creative thoughts start popping up. Thoughts I didn't have before, which contribute to solutions I ponder. On the back of this, I don't take my phone to the gym anymore. Nor do I think that my wireless router requires that extra add-on that extends its range to the living room.

From Saturday evening to Monday morning, I turn my phone off completely. I'm not available and can't call anyone or make spontaneous plans. I must ask people for directions. I can't take photos of the kids. I can't check football scores and so on. But I also notice this: without the news, I'm not tempted to get worked up about things beyond my control. Google Maps might have shown me the way to the cinema. But Google Maps wouldn't have explained why I might benefit from watching a particular movie. Instead of taking pictures, I cherish the unique moments. I don't hear job updates from colleagues or celebrity news. But I remember I haven't talked to an old friend in ages. (And then I make a note for Monday. I jot down all the things I want to do when the phone is back on.)

Does this sound silly? Is this silly?

Maybe. But I notice that the world's major religions all call for a day of rest each week or at specific times: Christianity has Sunday, Judaism the Sabbath, Islam has Friday, Buddhism its meditation times. The purpose of these rest periods is to step back, breathe, rest, reflect and so on. Perhaps turning off the phone one day a week is just the kind of break you need.

We're discussing all this in the context of self-knowledge. Self-knowledge is crucial. We need to understand what makes us happy, what drives us and what our long-term goals are. But we also need to understand what gets in our way and how the mechanisms that hinder us work. So, consider a designated spot to store your phone or tablet when you're not using it. When you're out and about, keep your phone at the bottom of your bag so you have to stop and rummage to find it. When waiting for the kettle to boil or a meeting to start, focus inward. Do a simple body exercise, stretch or breathing exercise. Notice the pattern of the floor. Are there pictures on the wall? Are they nice? Establish phone-free zones. Make it a rule not to take your smartphone to bed. When you wake up, try lying still for a moment instead of reaching for your phone.

SIGNPOST

It's 2 pm. You have a dentist appointment, and you're the first patient after lunch. Your appointment is at 2.30 pm, but the practice hasn't reopened yet. So, you're standing in the entrance area of the old building where your dentist works, alone and with no time pressure. And then it hits you: "Bummer, I've forgotten my phone at home."

While you wait in the stairwell, your frustration gives way to a budding interest. This staircase, with its deliberate elegance, is far more than just a connection between floors. What emotions and reactions did the architect intend to evoke with this design? Awe, tranquillity or perhaps a prompt for self-reflection? Gradually, the stairwell imparts a sense of calm. It's an unusual but invigorating feeling, this pause to simply be and think. You wonder, why don't I allow myself this luxury more often?

Choose the statements that resonate most with you:

- Social media can be a tool for connection. But it can also be a means of distracting from self-reflection or real-world relationships. It offers a curated reality, leading users to compare their lives to idealized versions of others and ignore the complexity and imperfection of their own lives.

- Throwing oneself into work is praised in many cultures. But, sometimes, it can be a way to avoid personal issues or the need for deeper self-examination. Busyness becomes a badge of honour, masking the avoidance of getting to know oneself better.
- The next purchase or the temporary satisfaction of acquiring new things can distract from deeper needs or dissatisfaction with one's life or self. This cycle of desire and gratification can become addictive, constantly diverting from inner emptiness.
- Immersing oneself in TV shows, films or streaming services for extended periods can be a form of escape from reality, responsibility or self-reflection. It offers an alternate universe where one can temporarily forget personal challenges or the need for growth.
- The compulsive consumption of news, information or educational content can be a sophisticated form of procrastination or avoidance, where the constant intake of new information serves as a barrier to reflecting on one's own life or making necessary changes.

On your way back from the dentist, you see children and parents at a playground. This should be a place where everyone has fun. But that's not the case for everyone: while some children are running around, laughing and having a great time, you see others who are angry because their sandcastle has collapsed, they can't get the shovel from the girl opposite or they have to wait too long for their turn on the slide.

Looking at the parents, you see the same mix of emotions. Some are laughing, pushing their children on swings or wheeling them along on the roundabout. But not everyone is having a good time. A mother is telling her children that she will leave without them if they don't come immediately (with a slightly too high pitch on 'immediately'). A father stands on the edge, looking bored at his phone.

You wonder why not everyone at the playground is happy. A place that should be all about fun. Maybe it's because of misplaced expectations. Children and parents come here hoping for the perfect day. In this perfect world, sandcastles don't fall apart. There are no little kids slowing down the big kids. The children are happy when mum says it's time to go home. And dad quietly hopes for a spot in the sun.

You wonder: "Where might I have misplaced expectations too?"

Do any of these thoughts sound familiar?

- Career and work: "I work hard and get good feedback, so I expect a pay rise or promotion soon."
- Relationships and love: "I put effort into my relationships, so I expect them to be strong and fulfilling."
- Personal achievements and success: "I set high goals and push myself, so I expect to achieve my goals and be recognized."
- Lifestyle and possessions: "I save and plan for the things I want, so I expect to have a comfortable lifestyle."
- Social life and friendships: "I am friendly and helpful to my friends, so I expect them to be there for me too."
- Health and fitness: "I eat healthily and stay active, so I expect to be less ill and have more energy for my family."
- Personal growth and happiness: "I work on myself and stay positive, so I expect to feel happy and fulfilled."
- Parenting and family life: "I give my family love and support, so I expect us to have a strong bond and happy moments together."

———————

This book aims to help you find your way to a prosperous 100-year life. In this chapter, we've discussed several key points:

First, we talked about Paul Dolan's idea of happiness. It's a practical idea that's neither superficial nor full of clichés.

Second, this chapter hopefully made it clear that only you can figure out what makes you happy. While there are some tips from science (like the importance of friends and family, health and access to nature), ultimately, you need to find out what brings you pleasure and purpose in life.

You also learned some tips on how to discover this, for instance, by paying attention to your daily experiences and not how you evaluate them.

Finally, this chapter hopefully showed you that all of this, while it may sound obvious, is hard to implement in daily life. Not just because we usually have so much to do but also because we live in a world full of distractions. Navigating these distractions is a crucial skill for a successful 100-year life.

We're approaching the end. Let's take a look at the future.

CHAPTER 7

LIVING WITH FORESIGHT: DEFINING WHAT MATTERS

Fred Hersch is one of the most successful contemporary pianists and composers. As a young boy growing up in Cincinnati, his innate musical talents quickly became evident. His parents supported him early on. But they weren't always helpful. His mother once remarked that his arms were too short for him to be a good pianist. It was a comment that triggered a series of self-limiting beliefs but also ignited the drive to defy expectations.

After high school, Hersch left his hometown to attend the country's best music school – in Boston. And from Boston, he frequently travelled to New York City to see bands perform in one of the city's jazz clubs.

One day, sitting in the audience of the legendary Vanguard Club in Manhattan, a mecca for jazz lovers, he formed a very concrete vision of his future self when seeing one of the pianists play in the club. This is from his autobiography: "I watched and studied the pianist, Harold Danko, a fine player in his late 20s, whom I had never heard before, and I thought: *I can do what he's doing. I could play here.*"[86]

He didn't just visualize his future self. He immediately acted after having seen it.

"At the end of the set, I went up to Danko and introduced myself. I wrote my name and number on a slip of paper and told him that if he ever needed a sub, he should call me. In my mind that night, I took my next step and moved to New York to set up shop as a working jazz musician."[87]

That night, he mentally relocated to New York. And soon after, the vision became a reality. Hersch moved to New York – the global capital of jazz.

His belief in his musical destiny was unwavering. Financial struggles were secondary in his pursuit of musical success. He hired band members and paid them each $100 without earning a cent himself. Money didn't matter to him as long as he felt he was on the right path.

He pestered club owners and fellow musicians. This is another section from his biography.

"At a jazz club called Bloomers ... I spotted Charlie Haden, one of the most important bassists in the history of jazz ... I went up to him and introduced myself. I said, 'Mr Haden, I love your music, and I know we're going to play together.' He looked me over like I was crazy, but I truly believed that it would happen."[88]

Hersch's debut album was called "Horizons." The title captures his philosophy, ambition and potential: he saw multiple paths ahead, each filled with possibilities.

Today, Hersch is revered in the jazz world. Of course, it's primarily his style that people love. His music is lyrical, nuanced and profoundly expressive. It's a unique and captivating sound. (Check out his interpretations of Jimmy Webb's "Wichita Lineman" or Billy Joel's "And So It Goes.")

I wonder how much of his success can be attributed to his ability to visualize his future self. Or his ability to see life as an arc. His memoirs illustrate the power of a long-term perspective. Our research at the Centre for Behavioural Research at Aegon shows that a deep connection with one's future self can significantly impact long-term success. Hersch's story is a lesson in the transformative power of this vision and a long-term mental time horizon.

CONNECTING WITH YOUR FUTURE SELF

Our research has also shown that people who have a strong connection with their future selves are in a better financial position. For example, individuals with the highest incomes who strongly identify with their future selves are six times more likely to save significant amounts for retirement than their high-earning peers who do not have such a connection to their future selves. Very similar patterns occur for the other income groups. And it's not just long-term savings. People with a strong and meaningful connection to their future selves typically have less debt. They are more likely to have money set aside for emergencies and transitions. They are more likely to possess critical illness coverage and life insurance. This shows that money alone is not enough. A strong connection with the future self is an important part of the money mindset.

The effects of having a long-term time horizon also extend to job satisfaction. People with a clear vision of their future selves enjoy their work more and find it more meaningful. They are not just earning money: they are working toward a future they have envisioned.

Emotionally, the benefits are equally clear. A strong connection with the future self correlates with fewer negative emotions such as frustration, despair, vulnerability and worry. Instead, these individuals often experience positive money emotions such as satisfaction, calmness, contentment and confidence.

This long-term perspective might explain part of Fred Hersch's success. His clear and vivid connection with his future self allowed him to navigate the competitive landscape of jazz music with determination and foresight. He saw himself not just as a musician in the present but as a significant contributor to the future jazz world. This vision drove him to practise diligently, proactively seek opportunities and connect with influential figures in the music scene. He was willing to forgo a better income in the beginning for long-term success. Costs and benefits in the present were not as important. The outcome in the long-term game was what mattered.

Who is your 'future self?' Does it feel a bit abstract to you? If so, you're not alone. Let's get a clearer vision.

OVERCOMING FUTURE HURDLES WITH SCENARIOS

Hal Hershfield, an American psychologist and behavioural scientist, made a fascinating discovery using fMRI scans (functional Magnetic Resonance Imaging, which maps brain activity).[89] He found that, when we think about our future selves, we activate brain areas typically involved when thinking about strangers. This could explain why it's so challenging to imagine our future selves – to our brain, it's like thinking about a stranger. And we wouldn't be more helpful, compassionate and kind to our future selves than we would be to any stranger on the street.

But what if we took a different starting point? Instead of first imagining our future *selves*, we start by imagining future *scenarios*.

Nava Ashraf, a behavioural economist at the London School of Economics, and her team of psychologists and economists explored this in a unique context.[90] They conducted a study with small business owners in Colombia. Many participants were female migrants from Venezuela, who had left their economically and socially devastated homeland to start anew elsewhere. Often, they had traumatic experiences during their journey to the neighbouring country (or even in their home country). Their success as small business owners would not only enable them to lead self-sufficient lives, but it would also have significant sociopolitical implications. Colombia has taken in many migrants from Venezuela and helping them to sustainably support themselves is in the state's interest.

The researchers' core assumption was that long-term success is more likely when one learns to vividly and emotionally imagine the future. Furthermore, they believed this ability could significantly improve the economic outcomes of entrepreneurs – especially compared to traditional business training methods that focus more on abstract thinking and cognition.

To systematically test their assumptions, the researchers recruited about 2,000 people who were randomly assigned to one of three groups. About 450 participants received no intervention or training, reflecting the reality of many businesspeople who operate without formal education. About 600 participants were enrolled in a training programme that taught traditional business skills like accounting, marketing and management. The remaining nearly 1,000 participants were placed in the so-called imagery programme group: this group received additional training on visualizing future scenarios alongside the standard business training.

One scenario presented to participants for visualization involved a vivid daily experience:

"Your alarm clock rings at 3 am. It's still dark and cold. You travel in your truck for an hour to get to Paloquemao's market. You arrive at the fish market. You can see and smell fresh fish piled up on top of the tables, with noisy salesmen. Think about this scene for a moment. I would like for you to paint an image or a video in your head, as if you were an artist or a film director trying to capture this moment. What do you see? What do you smell? How do you feel right now?"[91]

Visualizing an everyday scene, like the alarm ringing at 3 am and visiting a market, serves as a sort of mental rehearsal for the future business owners. By imagining these scenes, they could gradually develop concrete plans for their business ventures. For example, thinking through a typical market day led them to consider how they might present their products more effectively or interact with customers. They also imagined how they would tackle challenges such as getting up early and dealing with the long workday, the stress, and the hustle and bustle of a busy market. This type of visualization helps set realistic expectations for the business day and fosters the development of strategies to cope with these challenges.

Another scenario focused on the consequences of financial decisions:

"Imagine your entrepreneurial business works well and you receive a constant flow of profits. You feel satisfied and use your profits to cover personal expenses that you couldn't afford before. As you pay all these expenses, you forget to save. Six months later, you discover that one of your relatives or close friends gets sick. You need an emergency treatment that is awfully expensive. But you realize that you have no savings. What do you do? How do you feel in this situation? Is this a situation you could imagine happening in the future? How would this event affect your life in one year from now?"

The core of this exercise lies in the realization that, despite current business success and satisfaction, there is always the risk of unexpected events. Events that can cause significant financial strain. Through this exercise, participants should recognize the importance of saving for emergencies and planning ahead, even in times of success. By putting themselves in this situation, aspiring business owners learn to consider the consequences of their financial decisions, using the scenario to reflect on their attitude toward saving and financial preparedness. The questions at the end of the exercise aim to explore the emotional and long-term impacts of such decisions, thereby raising awareness for balanced and forward-looking financial planning.

What were the results of the study?

Well – you won't be surprised anymore. The study ran for about a year. The first follow-up was conducted at six to eight months, and the second 12 to 14 months after the end of the training program. The results showed that the imagery group, which participated in the training, achieved significantly better economic outcomes than the placebo group, which received only traditional business training. The success measurement was based on an index that included income, business survival, safety nets, business behaviour and investments. Specifically, income and business sales were considered, as well as whether the person was running an active business.

The study results are clear: long-term thinking, combined with the power of emotional and cognitive processing, is not only learnable but a key to lasting success.

This insight is groundbreaking. It proves that long-term progress goes beyond mere factual knowledge. Rather, success unfolds in the connection of this knowledge with emotional processes and the ability to vividly visualize. It's not just about learning technical skills but about the ability to envision future scenarios and understand emotional reactions to them.

Fred Hersch is an example of how the combination of technical skills (in his case, the ability to master the piano and his knack for beautiful harmonies) and the visualization of concrete future scenarios lead to long-term success. He saw himself on the stage at the Vanguard Club. He envisioned performing with other renowned musicians, imagining the success and recognition he would achieve in the jazz world. Just as the study participants used visualization to plan their business success, Hersch used his experiences to map out his musical journey, connecting his present actions with his future aspirations.

This insight also allows us to draw conclusions on how to plan for our long lives. It shows us that the key to long-term success lies in linking emotion and cognition when contemplating both the present and the future. Throughout this book, we've emphasized this connection – not least in the Signposts. Later on, in the final Signpost, you will find two scenarios inspired by Ashraf's research.

DEVELOPING A CLEAR VISION OF THE FUTURE

Hal Hershfield's research shows that if you see your future self as someone who is, deep down, similar to you, you're more likely to make decisions that are beneficial in the long run. Hershfield also demonstrates that you're likely to make better choices if you can clearly and positively envision your future self.[92] For example, imagine you're older and need money for future activities you enjoy, such as further education or taking a sabbatical. If you can clearly imagine this future, you're more likely to decide to save money now for the future rather than spending it on immediate pleasures.

Again, the musician Fred Hersch is a prime example of how to embody self-continuity effectively. When he pictured his future self, he recognized the deep connection to his present self, embodying a strong sense of continuity. Visiting jazz clubs in New York City and performing on big stages wasn't merely a distant dream for him; it was a natural progression aligned with his forward-looking vision. When he chose to pay band members out of his own pocket, earning nothing himself, he viewed it as an investment in his future self rather than just a current expense. This sense of connection and continuity between his present and future self was crucial for his sustained commitment. It wasn't just about having a dream or goal, but consistently aligning his present actions toward that envisioned future.

What does this mean for us? To be able to connect with our future selves, it really is rather important, too, to understand who we are right now. By gaining that understanding of what gives us pleasure and purpose, we can better imagine what we may enjoy doing later. This makes it easier to make choices that help us in the long run. So, taking the time to understand yourself today is key to making decisions that support your future.

In the insights about what brings you pleasure and purpose, you might also recognize 'deeper centres,' as Stephen Covey called them.[93] For example, you might find that you are primarily family-centred, partner-centred, work-centred, money-centred, pleasure-centred, environment-centred, self-centred and so on. This understanding of centres helps you shape a future self that aligns with your deeper values. For instance, if you are primarily family-centred, your vision of your future self might include being a supportive and engaged family member. If you are work-centred, success, achievement and diligence might play a larger role. Understanding these centres can help you make decisions and set long-term goals that are in harmony with your true self, both now and in the future.

THE PROSPECTIVE HINDSIGHT APPROACH

Hal Hershfield's research reveals the profound impact that visualizing your future self can have on decision-making. One of his most well-known studies involved participants being shown digitally and artificially aged images of themselves.[94] This simple confrontation with a photo of their future selves led to an increase in their retirement savings rates. This outcome, in turn, showed how connecting with the future self can motivate better actions today.

Perhaps unsurprisingly, the implications of this mindset extend beyond financial planning. Hershfield's work shows that this practice also has tangible benefits for health and personal development. For instance, people who could vividly imagine their future selves were more likely to make healthier lifestyle choices. Makes sense, right?

Building on this, several concrete techniques have been developed to enhance the visualization of the future self. One such technique is writing letters to and from your future self. One letter begins, "Dear future self ..." The other begins, "Dear past self ..." This exercise encourages individuals to articulate their future goals, fears and aspirations. By writing to their future selves, people can express their hopes and expectations (and also their worries and fears). Conversely, a fictional letter from the future self to the present can offer advice, wisdom or encouragement. This bidirectional communication fosters a deeper connection with the future self, making it more tangible and real.[95]

Another technique involves reinterpreting the perception of time. Thinking about the future in smaller units can make long-term goals seem more tangible and achievable. Instead of thinking in years, think in days. This brings the distant future into a clearer, more understandable perspective. It enhances the sense of urgency and importance associated with future-oriented decisions. For instance, if you want to lose weight or run a marathon, break your training plan into daily tasks and achievements. Instead of seeing it as a multi-year effort, view each day as a step toward your goal. This daily focus can boost your motivation and make the process more manageable.

Through such techniques, visualizing the future self becomes accessible and practical. 'The future' can feel pretty vague and nebulous. By anchoring it in concrete, actionable practices, you open up a way to actively engage with your future self. And this can lead to more thoughtful and future-oriented decisions in the present.

The Prospective Hindsight approach, developed at our Centre for Behavioural Research, is also strongly inspired by Hal Hershfield. It is based on imagining a future situation and then working backward. Here's a guide to carrying out this method.

THE PROSPECTIVE HINDSIGHT APPROACH

Step 1: Personal Information
- Your current age: _____
- Your partner's current age (if applicable): _____
- Your children's current ages (if applicable): _____
- How many years into the future would you like to think? Choose between 3, 5, 10, 15 or 20 years.

Step 2: Visualizing the Future
- In __ years, you will be: _____
- (If applicable) Your partner will be: _____
- (If applicable) Your children will be: _____

How do you feel when you think about this future? Are you excited, anxious, curious, hopeful, uncertain, nostalgic?

Step 3: Diving into the Future
Next, dive into the future time point you chose in Step 1. The goal is to create a concrete picture of what the future might look like. Here are some guiding questions to help you.

Future Living Situation:
In __ years, I want to live in _____ (country) in _____ (a small house, bungalow, semi-detached house, apartment, hotel, caravan, etc.), and it will be in _____ (a rural village, the mountains, city, small town, etc.).

Companions:
I want to live _____ (alone, with my family, with my partner, with my children, with friends). There _____ (will/won't) be a pet.

Time Investment:
I want to spend more time with _____.

Work:
In a typical week, I will _____ (work full-time, work part-time, freelance, not work) and I want to _____ (support my local community, do volunteer work, support family and friends, etc.).

Leisure Activities:
In my free time, I will _____ (spend time in nature, watch or play sports, pursue a hobby or interest, spend time with family and friends).

Financial Goals:
In __ years, I want to have enough money to _____ (eat at nice restaurants, renovate my home, go on holidays abroad, build a financial cushion, support my family, start a new career training, donate to charity, take a study sabbatical).

Personal Fulfilment:
Something that will seem important to me in __ years is _____ (career success, further education, time with family, community engagement, taking care of my health and wellbeing).

Achievements:
Something I want to have achieved in the next __ years is _____.

Advice from the Future:
My financial advice from the future to my present self: _____.
My life advice from the future to my present self: _____.

Step 4: Reflect

After you've considered these questions and thought about them, reflect on your feelings: do you feel excited, hopeful or inspired? Or maybe anxious, uncertain or even overwhelmed? Perhaps your present self feels guilty toward your future self?

Remember, your emotions have a positive intent. They hopefully inform your decisions. It's normal to have mixed feelings when thinking about the future. Every emotion you feel should be taken seriously and can help you understand your deeper desires and concerns.

The most crucial question is: are you on the right path to live this life? Are you taking steps today that lead you toward this future? Or do you find that your current path diverges from this vision? This is a decisive moment of reflection – it's about aligning your current actions with your future aspirations. Remember, the journey to your future begins with the steps you take today.

Step 5: Anticipate Obstacles

The final step of our prospective hindsight is based on the pre-mortem technique, which invites you to anticipate potential future challenges. It's about imagining what could go wrong before it does. The purpose is simple yet profound: to identify possible obstacles in advance so you can proactively take measures to avoid or mitigate them.

In this phase, we encourage you to consider two different types of factors: those *within* your control and those *beyond* your control. This approach aligns with the principles of Cognitive Behavioural Therapy (CBT). It's rooted in ancient Stoic philosophy. Reflect on the following questions. They are not meant as a checklist but as a guide to thoughtful introspection and strategic planning.

First, ask yourself:

"What external factors could prevent me from achieving my desired future?" These could include job loss, changes in financial markets, health issues or legal changes. Recognizing these factors helps you understand and accept life's uncertainties.

Then consider:

"What personal factors could stop me from achieving my future goals?"
Think about aspects like health and wellbeing, saving, future planning and your understanding of what brings you happiness. Acknowledging these factors empowers you to make changes and take control of your journey.

Finally:

"What steps can I take now to address these challenges?"
This might include developing healthier routines, higher savings rates, spending more time with the kids, seeking advice or simply dedicating more time to what fulfils you. By identifying actionable steps, you can start making a positive impact on your future today.

———————————

SIGNPOST

Imagine a day ten years from now: you walk into your local supermarket, surrounded by the hum of fridges and the murmur of other shoppers. In the fruit and vegetable section, you ponder whether to go for organic produce or the regular stuff, swayed by offers and prices. In the bakery aisle, you wonder if you should opt for wholegrains for health benefits or treat yourself to a fancy pastry. When you get to household goods, you're deciding between eco-friendly products or cheaper alternatives. At the checkout, you reflect on your purchases, feeling relaxed and secure as you place your items on the conveyor belt.

Think about this scene for a moment. Imagine how you'd capture this moment as a film director. How do you feel during this shopping trip – relaxed, content, financially secure? Visualize this experience in your mind.

Now picture this: you've been working reliably for the same employer for years. One morning, after a quick coffee break, you return to your desk, ready to tackle the day's tasks. But instead of diving into routine work, you find an email from your boss with the subject line 'Important Company Update.' Opening the message, you learn that your job is at risk due to economic difficulties and company restructuring. It's not entirely unexpected; there have been hints. But now it's certain.

What would you do first? How would you feel at that moment? Are you prepared for such a turn of events? Is this a scenario you can imagine in your future? How would this event impact your life in a year?

To wrap up this chapter, let's revisit another story from Fred Hersch's biography, *Good Things Happen Slowly: A Life in and out of Jazz.* The title itself beautifully encapsulates the lessons we've explored in this third part of the book.

In his biography, Hersch recounts how once a year he and his manager would work on a BAWL – that's a 'Big Ass Wish List.' It isn't a list like any other. A BAWL is a collection of grand dreams and aspirations, unfettered by the constraints of practicality. One year, Hersch expressed a desire to compose a large-scale work setting Walt Whitman's poetry to music. This project, inspired by his deep admiration for the poet, aimed to capture the essence of Whitman's celebration of human connection and the natural world. It was a far-reaching and ambitious dream, perfect for the BAWL. And guess what happened. A few months later, Hersch got a call from his manager with incredible news: three performances of this yet-to-be-composed piece were already scheduled for the following year.

Did Fred Hersch just get lucky?

Of course not. We've discussed the importance of self-knowledge in a long life in previous chapters. It's about recognizing what drives us, finding time for self-reflection and having a clear vision of our future.

Hersch's success with his BAWL demonstrates the significance of taking time to contemplate our aspirations and understanding what gives us pleasure and purpose. Hersch's project wasn't just a musical endeavour but a profound alignment with his joys and goals. His BAWL was a vision of his future self, imagining possibilities beyond the present.

Let me clarify: Fred Hersch's BAWL isn't about setting sky-high, unrealistic goals or blindly 'following your dreams' with the expectation that success will just magically happen. That kind of 'mindset advice' ('just follow your dreams and anything can happen') can be pretty dangerous. It sets you up for disappointment when things don't go as planned or, well ... dreamed. Instead, I like to think of the BAWL as your personal compass. Just as Seneca said, "He who does not know where he is sailing will never catch the right wind," having that type of wish list helps you dream big while staying grounded, ensuring your goals are both ambitious and achievable.

There's also something to be said in defence of 'following your dream:' following your dreams doesn't necessarily set you up for failure. Or rather, it isn't necessarily less likely to set you up for failure than 'playing it safe.' Playing it safe doesn't guarantee you'll avoid disappointment or regret, especially in a world where industries, technologies and social contexts are constantly evolving. Following your dreams isn't about guaranteed success; it's about giving yourself the chance to engage in something meaningful and enjoyable.

Moreover, anticipation can play a crucial role in a happy life. As Paul Dolan explains in *Happiness by Design*, increasing the number of positive experiences in our lives is what it's all about. While anticipation can bring both excitement and anxiety, focusing on the positive aspects can keep us motivated and eagerly looking forward to our goals. Differently put, it's a positive experience.

By paying attention to what we dream about, we learn a lot about ourselves. These dreams reveal our deeper desires and values, giving us insights that we can use to make smarter decisions about how we earn, spend and manage our money. When our financial choices reflect what truly makes us happy, we embrace the concept of prosperity, creating a life that's not only successful but also deeply fulfilling.

Hersch's experience is proof that self-knowledge is far more than just introspective reflection; it's a way to unlock more in life.

Simply put, self-knowledge is an asset!

Let's conclude.

FINALLY, A PLAN

Let's start with a quick recap of the core issues in this book before I present a financial plan that funds a happy long life.

Right at the start, we looked at the decisions of Dr Ingmar Zöller (the eye doctor who decided to become an S-Bahn driver), Emily Hanley (the copywriter who lost her job to ChatGPT), Martina Rosenberg (the freelancer wondering when her mother, in need of care, would finally pass away), and Oliver Noelting (the software developer who did everything for early retirement until his daughter was born).

Their considerations, which preceded their decisions, exemplified the challenges of a 100-year life.

- Do I keep my job for the financial security it offers – even though the work doesn't fulfil me?
- Should I pursue further education or training? Or can I still find success with my existing skills and knowledge?
- How do I balance caring for my parents with the need to earn money today and be there for my children?
- Is it worth working more and earning more today if it means missing out on precious time with my baby daughter?

Essentially, these considerations boil down to weighing financial security today against financial security tomorrow. And balancing the happy life today against the happy life tomorrow.

These are incredibly tough considerations.

Many of us end up making the wrong decisions: often choosing the status quo. We opt for the easier path to avoid immediate pain. We dislike our daily lives due to multiple stresses. And we later regret not having done what would have made us happier in the long term.

It's understandable why this happens: Daniel Kahneman and Amos Tversky, considered the founders of modern behavioural science, discovered that people often don't evaluate their lives based on their overall and long-term wellbeing, but on gains or losses relative to a 'neutral' reference point. Many of us stay in a disliked job because it's easier to stick with what we know or because we fear potential loss if we make a change. Or because we want to avoid the effort involved in making changes.

We refuse further education because we believe that the investments we made in the past "must have been worth something." This stops us from exploring new paths. If it would be better to step back and take more care of our parents, we realize we don't have any savings, simply because we live in an environment where no one else built such savings either. The thought, "None of my friends or colleagues have savings, so I don't need any!" influences our financial decisions. We focus not on what makes us happy in the long run, but often on false reference points: the status quo, sunk costs, social norms and so on.

In this book, I've argued that we need self-knowledge for better decisions.

Self-knowledge about various things:

- Self-knowledge about which attitudes, beliefs, emotional reactions, cognitive biases or habits lead us to certain decisions and actions.
- Self-knowledge about where these things might come from – either from our own past or from human evolution.
- Self-knowledge about what is important to us today, what was important to us in the past and, accordingly, what is likely to be important to us in the future.

- Self-knowledge about the things, activities and experiences that give us pleasure and purpose in life today.
- Self-knowledge about the needs, desires and necessities of our future selves.
- Self-knowledge about how the reality of everyday life, with all its distractions (media, digital technologies, various demands), prevents us from thinking about the things that really matter.

Without this self-knowledge, the 100-year life can quickly become a trap. We stay in jobs we dislike. We make decisions about further education too late. We are not mentally prepared for crises. And we regret not having experienced more unique moments consciously.

The danger of falling into a trap is real. We fall into a trap when we stick to the financial and life planning of a three-stage life, instead of adapting to the realities of a longer and more complex multistage life. We prefer to cling to old patterns:

- We don't save enough for transition periods, making it harder to change career paths or take longer breaks.
- We mistakenly assume that our most productive years are in the middle of life, which often results in sacrifices in family life, health and overall wellbeing.
- The fear of giving up a well-paid job stops us from seeking more fulfilling professions.
- The reluctance to take pay cuts for further education during the mid-life stage blocks our personal growth.
- Overemphasis on saving for the future often comes at the expense of enjoying the present.

These beliefs and strategies lead us into a trap where our long life doesn't result in either long-term happiness or security.

To enjoy the benefits of a 100-year life, we should recognize the flexibility of our life stages: leisure, education and productive years can be distributed differently.

For example, Oliver decided to reduce his working hours to spend more time with his daughter. Meetings, emails, projects – all these professional commitments can be fulfilled later in life. But the unique moments with his daughter can only be experienced now. In five years, she'll be going to school, ten years later she'll be a teenager, and in 20 years she'll be leading her own life. The precious moments of childhood can only be experienced in the present. Dr Zöller realized that life is too short to waste in a job he didn't love. He chose less money but more personal fulfilment.

Why don't more people take this step?

Funding such a life is, of course, a challenge. But, ultimately, it's mostly *mental barriers* that hold us back. That's the main premise of this book. If we realign our attitudes and expectations about life and work, we can unlock the full benefits of a 100-year life.

In the second chapter, we talked about the 50–30–20 rule of thumb. As a reminder: 50% of income goes to essential expenses, 30% to personal wants and needs and 20% to improving the financial situation. If there's bad debt, 20% of the income is used to pay it off. If savings for emergencies or transitions are insufficient, they are built up; otherwise, the money is saved for retirement and possible transition periods.

Even with such financial planning, job loss like Emily's and transition periods like Martina's remain emotionally challenging. But at least such planning provides us with financial security and reduces some of the stress factors. It gives us a bit of slack.

The 50–30–20 rule of thumb also offers a balanced perspective on how we manage our time and the gift of a longer, healthier life. This rule helps us balance our spending and investments across different time horizons:

- Fifty per cent of income is spent on present needs. This includes daily expenses like maintenance, heating and food. These costs are immediate and essential for our day-to-day life here and now.
- The 30% for personal wants are also anchored in the present. This covers spending on leisure activities like going out, holidays and hobbies. While these expenses are made in the present, they are also long-term investments in personal relationships, family and enriching experiences that can benefit us in the long run.
- The remaining 20% for improving the financial situation has a long-term perspective. Paying off debt deals with past financial decisions, while building up savings is about future expenses. Saving for transitions and retirement focuses on the distant future.

This rule of thumb also promotes 'balanced gratification,' which we discussed in the chapter '100-year Life Happiness.' It allows us to lead a fulfilling life not just in the present but also in the long term. By distributing our resources in this balanced way, we can enjoy the present while being prepared for future challenges.

However, it's important that the 50–30–20 rule is handled flexibly, depending on our current life situation. During periods of unemployment or when we're living off our savings for other reasons, the rule can be adjusted, for example, to 70–25–5. Here, spending on basic needs and personal wants is given more weight, while less is put aside for long-term financial security (or can be). Once we enter a more productive phase of life, the proportions can be adjusted again, for instance, to 50–20–30, to focus more on improving the financial situation. When we are in a stable phase, we return to the classic 50–30–20 distribution. By applying this rule flexibly, we can ensure we are well-prepared both in the present and in future phases of life.

THE FINANCIAL PLAN FOR A 100-YEAR LIFE

The financial plan presented here offers a comprehensive overview. It embeds financial decisions within the overall context of the desired lifestyle. It highlights that effective financial planning isn't just about numbers; at its core, it's about funding a happy and long life.

This financial plan should make it easier to make complex decisions, as it aligns our financial situation with our personal values and goals. Thus, we can make decisions that make financial sense and ensure long-term quality of life.

This is a holistic and personal plan. I have filled it out as an example. Use it as a template for yourself – tailor it to your needs and circumstances.

The clear listing of savings, investments, assets (what you own), and liabilities and debts (what you owe) provides a transparent overview of your net worth. "There is no more important first step to controlling your money life than building a personal balance sheet," says Brian Portnoy.[96]

MY FINANCIAL PLAN

PART 1: ME

My Centres or Life Priorities:
- Work-Life Balance: I want to reconcile my professional and personal life so that both career success and hobbies are possible.
- My Partner: I want to maintain a strong, loving relationship, characterized by understanding and shared happy moments.

What gives me pleasure and purpose today:
- Project X, because it challenges my creativity and technical knowledge.
- Evenings with the kids, because they help me unwind from work stress.

What might give me pleasure and purpose later:
In the next 18 months, I will go out with friends more often, build a conservatory and find time for swimming.

My future self:
In five years, I want to have started a small company specializing in sustainable technologies.

In ten years, I want to slow down a bit, work only part time and have time to write novels.

Money Mindset:
I tend to be a bit odd with money because I save excessively out of fear of not having enough for unforeseen events.

Therefore, I need to focus more on enjoying life by investing in experiences that bring me joy.

PART 2: MY FINANCES

My Net Worth:

Emergency Fund:	£5,500
Transition Fund:	£15,000
Retirement Savings:	£112,000
Assets (property, jewellery):	£220,000
Debts (mortgage, student loan, credit cards):	-£163,000

Net Worth:	£189,500

My Net Income: £3,000
I Spend It On:
50% on necessities
25% on wants
25% on improving my financial situation

I find this appropriate because I plan to reduce my working hours soon and thus want to build higher savings.

It also considers how to allocate monthly income most effectively: how much for necessities, how much for wants, how much for improving the financial situation. In this case, it's not 50–30–20, but there's a good reason for it.

But this plan integrates personal life goals and values – in this example, work-life balance and maintaining relationships – into the financial strategy. It connects financial metrics with what makes life meaningful and enjoyable.

Additionally, it takes a forward-looking perspective, with a clear vision for the coming years – in this example, starting a business. This helps in viewing current decisions in light of long-term goals and planning accordingly.

This plan also invites self-reflection. In this example, the tendency to over-save is acknowledged, concluding that finding a balance that addresses both current needs and future goals is essential.

The subtitle of this book promises to fund a long, happy life. Hopefully, it has become clear that true prosperity is not achieved solely through money. Yes, money is important. Without money, it's difficult to live well. But it's also about understanding what we really want. Ignoring this was the great mistake of the Buddenbrooks. Despite their objective high levels of wealth, they made life hard and miserable for themselves. (And, ironically, as a consequence, they also squandered their wealth.) Therefore, it's important to pay attention to what gives us meaning and joy in life, as well as to understand and control our emotions and thoughts. We need more emotional intelligence! Because – perhaps I say this too often – leading a happy, long and financially secure life is more of a *mental challenge*. It is a financial challenge only in the second place.

The life and financial plan presented here also encourages you to consider your priorities for the next 18 months.[97] Why might a relatively short-term focus be beneficial in an era where we might live to 100?

In a century-long life, the focus naturally tends to be on the distant future. That's a necessity, no doubt. However, it's equally essential to recognize the value of short-term planning. First, because we don't only live in the future, but also today. And happiness lost now is happiness lost forever – in the words of Paul Dolan. Second, it's about training our focus on what brings us pleasure and purpose in life. This is a skill we need to learn as it rarely comes to us naturally. Having objectives in the near future – something we intentionally and purposefully will spend money on – will train us to become better spenders, too.

Take retirement, for example. Many people are looking forward to it. They dream of early retirement. They believe that once they retire, everything will be easy. But the reality is more nuanced. While retirement can reduce work-related stress and provide more free time, it also brings challenges that many don't anticipate. According to Rosenthal and Moore,[98] retirement is one of life's most stressful events, often leading to feelings of aimlessness and social isolation. Health outcomes vary: some retirees enjoy better mental health and increased physical activity, while others face higher risks of chronic illnesses and loneliness. Early or involuntary retirement can exacerbate these issues, highlighting the importance of planning not just for the long term, but also addressing immediate needs and building a fulfilling daily routine.

A 100-year life isn't just about retirement; it's also about career choices, lifelong learning and personal development. But generally speaking, without the ability to focus on what brings us pleasure and purpose, it's challenging to lead a happy life.

Another reason for short-term planning is the creation of happy memories. By intentionally creating moments of joy and satisfaction in the next 18 months, we collect valuable memories that will enrich us long term. These memories will hopefully serve as a source of joy and inspiration long after the moments have passed. They enhance our lives in ways that extend beyond the immediate moment and can strengthen us during difficult times.

In short, a 100-year life is not just about the future. It's also about today. Or the other way around: it's not just about today, but also about the future.

Now, one last point before we wrap up for good. A point that Daniel Crosby mentioned in his foreword: it's not just about you. Yes, we've developed *your* financial plan, which considers *your* financial situation, what brings *you* pleasure and purpose in the short, medium and long term, your money mindset and so on. We also talked about your future *self*.

Ideally, though, you won't navigate your 100-year life alone, but with close companions: your family, friends, a life partner and other valuable social connections. The Harvard Study of Adult Development, one of the longest-running studies of its kind, shows that the quality of interpersonal relationships is the strongest indicator of healthy ageing. George Vaillant, who led the study for three decades, emphasised in his book, *Aging Well*, that stable and supportive relationships most significantly contribute to long-term wellbeing. People who were satisfied with their relationships at age 50 were healthier at age 80.

That's why the path to happiness and wellbeing in a 100-year life is accompanied by strong and supportive companions. Your path to prosperity considers those close to you, too.

I wish you – and yours! – all the best of luck!

Or, rather: balanced gratification.

NOTES

1. For example, in https://www.zeit.de/2023/34/berufswechsel-lokfuehrer-augenarzt or: https://www.berliner-zeitung.de/mensch-metropole/ingmar-zoeller-berlin-s-bahn-gleiswechsel-warum-ein-augenarzt-jetzt-s-bahnen-durch-berlin-steuert-li.429707

2. https://www.businessinsider.de/karriere/international-career/ich-habe-job-an-chat-gpt-verloren-arbeite-jetzt-in-einem-supermarkt/

3. Rosenberg, Martina: Mutter, wann stirbst du endlich? Wenn die Pflege der kranken Eltern zur Zerreißprobe wird. München: Blanvalet Taschenbuch Verlag, 2014

4. Allen, James: *The Path of Prosperity*. New York: R. F. Fenno, 1907

5. Gratton, Lynda; Scott, Andrew J.: *The 100-Year Life: Living and Working in an Age of Longevity.* London: Bloomsbury Publishing, 2016

6. Oliver's story has been published in these German outlets: https://www.spiegel.de/familie/rente-mit-40-und-frugalismus-mit-weniger-geld-zum-gluecklicheren-leben-a-ff697155-2393-4291-8b8d-21a9a090d88e or here: https://urldefense.com/v3/__https://www.stern.de/wirtschaft/geld/frugalismus--er-wollte-mit-40-jahren-in-rente-gehen---dann-kam-das-leben-dazwischen-30689442.html__;!!LTKUihUYLQ!Imbe4jKOZmdeKAlt6WeD8TV3_UAAAqKcqdRN8trvlO6dPwgoe-PDzYPsYxFZ_9WruhlYng9G5XtPvw7EawLptek2$

7. Credit where credit is due: I took this idea from Paul Armson's book *Enough? How Much Money Do You Need for the Rest of Your Life*. Scotts Valley: CreateSpace Independent Publishing Platform, 2016.

8. Mann, Thomas (1921): *Buddenbrooks. The Decline of A Family.* London: Martin Secker Ltd. p531

9. Crosby, Daniel: *Soul of Wealth*, p51. Petersfield: Harriman House, 2024

10. Padley, Matt; Shepherd, Claire (2021): "Retirement living standards in the UK in 2021." Loughborough University, Centre for Research in Social Policy, 2021. https://urldefense.com/v3/__https://www.retirementlivingstandards.org.uk/Retirement-living-standards-in-the-UK-in-2021.pdf__;!!LTKUihUYLQ!Imbe4jKOZmdeKAlt6WeD8TV3"_UAAAqKcqdRN8trvlO6dPwgoe-PDzYPsYxFZ_9WruhlYng9G5XtPvw7Ea2l9gFBm$

11. Padley, Matt; Shepherd, Claire (2021): "Retirement living standards in the UK in 2021." Loughborough University, Centre for Research in Social Policy, 2021. https://urldefense.com/v3/__https://www.retirementlivingstandards.org.uk/Retirement-living-standards-in-the-UK-in-2021.pdf__;!!LTKUihUYLQ!Imbe4jKOZmdeKAlt6WeD8TV3_UAAAqKcqdRN8trvlO6dPwgoe-PDzYPsYxFZ_9WruhlYng9G5XtPvw7Ea2l9gFBm$, S. 22

12. Padley, Matt; Shepherd, Claire (2021): "Retirement living standards in the UK in 2021." Loughborough University, Centre for Research in Social Policy, 2021. https://urldefense.com/v3/__https://www.retirementlivingstandards.org.uk/Retirement-living-standards-in-the-UK-in-2021.pdf__;!!LTKUihUYLQ!Imbe4jKOZmdeKAlt6WeD8TV3_UAAAqKcqdRN8trvlO6dPwgoe-PDzYPsYxFZ_9WruhlYng9G5XtPvw7Ea2l9gFBm$, S. 11

13. Kahneman, Daniel; Deaton, Angus: "High income improves evaluation of life but not emotional wellbeing." Proceedings of the National Academy of Sciences, 2010. 107(38), 16489–16493. DOI: 10.1073/pnas.1011492107

14. https://gutezitate.com/zitat/237796

15. Ashraf, Nava; Karlan, Dean; Yin, Wesley: Tying Odysseus to the Mast: Evidence From a Commitment Savings Product in the Philippines, The Quarterly Journal of Economics, Volume 121, Ausgabe 2, Mai 2006. S. 635–672, https://urldefense.com/v3/__https://doi.org/10.1162/qjec.2006.121.2.635__;!!LTKUihUYLQ!Imbe4jKOZmdeKAlt6WeD8TV3_UAAAqKcqdRN8trvlO6dPwgoe-PDzYPsYxFZ_9WruhlYng9G5XtPvw7Eayz96GMV$

16. In case this sounds like jargon, and for full transparency: we're keeping money from our transition funds in Vanguard's LifeStrategy® 60% Equity Fund.

17. Benz, Christine: *How to Retire: 20 Lessons for a Happy, Successful, and Wealthy Retirement*. London: Harriman House, 2024

18. Housel, Morgan: *The Psychology of Money: Timeless Lessons on Wealth, Greed and Happiness*. London: Harriman House, 2020

19. Widger, Charles; Crosby, Daniel: *Personal Benchmark: Integrating Behavioral Finance and Investment Management*. Hoboken: Wiley, 2014

20. Ramit Sethi on The Long-View Podcast (2023): "Ramit Sethi: Investing shouldn't be your identity". https://www.morningstar.com/personal-finance/ramit-sethi-investing-shouldnt-be-your-identity

21. Gerd Gigerenzer makes this point in his book: *Risk Savvy: How to Make Good Decisions*. New York: Penguin Books, 2014

22. Warren, Elizabeth; Tyagi, Amelia Warren: *All Your Worth: The Ultimate Lifetime Money Plan*. New York: Free Press, 2006

23. Unpublished research conducted by Aegon's Centre for Behavioural Research.

24. According to the FCA, approximately 34% of UK adults have either no savings or less than £1,000 in a savings account, equating to around 22.8 million people with minimal financial reserves. https://www.money.co.uk/savings-accounts/savings-statistics

25. As of August 2024, the average credit card debt per household stood at £2,518, https://themoneycharity.org.uk/money-statistics/ and about 1 in 10 confess they "owe too much debt" considering their household's income situation. Aegon Financial Wellbeing Index, https://aegon.theapsgroup.scot/Financial-wellbeing-2024/14/

26. According to the ONS, the median pension pot size for individuals aged 55–64 in the UK is approximately £107,300. This figure is significantly lower than a recommended amount for a comfortable retirement. https://www.ons.gov.uk/peoplepopulationandcommunity/personalandhouseholdfinances/incomeandwealth/bulletins/pensionwealthingreatbritain/latest

27. Housel, Morgan: *The Psychology of Money: Timeless Lessons on Wealth, Greed, and Happiness*. Petersfield: Harriman House, 2020, S. 13 - 25

28. Peters, Steve: *My Hidden Chimp*. London: Lagom, 2023

29. Kahnemann, Daniel: *Thinking, Fast and Slow*. London: Penguin Books, 2011

30. Mullainathan, Sendhil; Shafir, Eldar: *Scarcity: Why Having Too Little Means So Much*. London: Penguin, 2014

31. Crosby, Daniel: *Behavioural Investor*. Petersfield: Harriman House, 2018. p118

32. Crosby, Daniel: *Behavioural Investor*. Petersfield: Harriman House, 2018. p62

33. Burnett, Dean: *Emotional Ignorance: Lost and Found in the Science of Emotion*. London: Guardian Faber, 2023

34. Graeber, David: *Debt: The First 5,000 Years*. Brooklyn, NY: Melville House, 2011

35. Harari, Yuval Noah: *Sapiens – A Brief History of Humankind*. New York: Harper, 2015

36. Unlike Harari, I don't think money is a social construct. Money isn't valuable only because we collectively agreed it is. Because we accepted its value, we acted (and act) accordingly. And these actions have tangible, material consequences. It shaped economies, built cities, and determined who thrived and who struggled.

37. "Cash for Kids. Why policies to boost birth rates don't work." London: *The Economist*, 25 May 2024. S. 9

38. Deutsche Rentenversicherung: Die Geschichte der Deutschen Rentenversicherung. Berlin: Online: https://urldefense.com/v3/__https://www. deutsche-rentenversicherung.de/DRV/DE/Ueber-uns-und-Presse/Historie/ historie_detailseite.html__;!!LTKUihUYLQ!lmbe4jKOZmdeKAlt6WeD8TV3_ UAAAqKcqdRN8trvlO6dPwgoe-PDzYPsYxFZ_9WruhlYng9G5XtPvw7Ea6BoPjej$

39. Office of National Statistics: Estimates of the very old, including centenarians, UK: 2002 to 2019. London: Online: https://urldefense.com/v3/ __https://www.ons.gov.uk/peoplepopulationandcommunity/ birthsdeathsandmarriages/ageing/bulletins/estimatesoftheveryoldincluding centenarians/2002to2019__;!!LTKUihUYLQ!lmbe4jKOZmdeKAlt6WeD8TV3_ UAAAqKcqdRN8trvlO6dPwgoe-PDzYPsYxFZ_9WruhlYng9G5XtPvw7Ea_qc T10M$, 2021

40. Jasilionis, Domantas; van Raalte, Alyson; Klüsener, Sebastian; Grigoriev, Pavel: "The underwhelming German life expectancy." *European Journal of Epidemiology*, 2023. DOI: 10.1007/s10654-023-00995-5

41. Woolf, Steven H.; Chapman, Derek A.; Buchanich, Jeanine M.; Bobby, Kimberley J.; Zimmerman, Elizabeth B.; Blackburn, Steven M.: "Changes in midlife death rates across racial and ethnic groups in the United States: systematic analysis of vital statistics." BMJ. 2018. https://urldefense.com/v3/__https://doi. org/10.1136/bmj.k3096__;!!LTKUihUYLQ!lmbe4jKOZmdeKAlt6WeD8TV3_ UAAAqKcqdRN8trvlO6dPwgoe-PDzYPsYxFZ_9WruhlYng9G5XtPvw7EawCmEgrT$.

Leon, David A; Jdanov, Dmitry; Shkolnikov, Vladimir M.: "Trends in life expectancy and age-specific mortality in England and Wales, 1970–2016, in comparison with a set of 22 high-income countries: an analysis of vital statistics data." London: *The Lancet*, 2019.

Case, Anne; Deaton, Angus. "Rising morbidity and mortality in midlife among white non-Hispanic Americans in the 21st century." Proceedings of the National Academy of Sciences of the United States of America. 2015;112(49):15078–83.

Child Poverty Action Group: The Austerity Generation. "The impact of a decade of cuts on family incomes and child poverty." London: Online: https://urldefense.com/v3/__https://cpag.org. uk/sites/default/files/files/Austerity*20Generation*20FINAL. pdf__;JSU!!LTKUihUYLQ!lmbe4jKOZmdeKAlt6WeD8TV3_ UAAAqKcqdRN8trvlO6dPwgoe-PDzYPsYxFZ_9WruhlYng9G5XtPvw7EaweP lJoV$, 2017

42. Hoffmann, Maren: Was muss sich ändern, damit wir länger arbeiten wollen? Hamburg: Der Spiegel, 2023. Online: https://www.spiegel.de/karriere/ ruhestand-was-muss-sich-aendern-damit-wir-laenger-arbeiten-wollen-a- 10a9b2fa-57bc-4ccc-b4dc-7312e46ad3fb

43. Moynes, Riley E.: *The Four Phases of Retirement. What to Expect When You're Retiring.* Riley E. Moynes, 2016

44. Levitin, Daniel: *The Changing Mind: A Neuroscientist's Guide to Ageing Well.* London: Penguin Life, 2021

45. Benz, Christine: *How to Retire. 20 Lessons for a Happy, Successful, and Wealthy Retirement.* Harriman House, Petersfield, UK

46. Benz, Christine: *How to Retire. 20 Lessons for a Happy, Successful, and Wealthy Retirement.* Harriman House, Petersfield, UK, p2

47. Scott, Andrew: *The Longevity Imperative. Building a Better Society for Healthier, Longer Lives.* London: Basic Books, 2024. S. 1-4

48. I appreciate there's a class dimension to consider, too. Teresa Ghilarducci, in her book, *Work, Retire, Repeat: The Uncertainty of Retirement in the New Economy*, argues that working-class and lower-middle-class individuals would be put at a disadvantage if they needed to work longer and retire earlier. They have more physically demanding jobs, resulting in worse health outcomes and reduced benefits from traditional retirement arrangements. There will also be a class bias in my argument for advocating for more breaks throughout working lives, as those in more strenuous and less secure employment may find it harder to take extended pauses without jeopardizing their financial stability.

49. Office of National Statistics: "Deaths registered in England and Wales: 2023": https://www.ons.gov.uk/peoplepopulationandcommunity/ birthsdeathsandmarriages/deaths/bulletins/deathsregistrationsummarytables/2023

50. Goldman, Lee: "Three stages of health encounters over 8,000 human generations and how they inform future public health." *American Journal of Public Health*, 2018

51. Bocquet-Appel, Jean-Pierre: "When the world's population took off: The springboard of the Neolithic demographic transition." Washington, DC: *Science*, vol. 333, no. 6042, 2011, S. 560-561

52. Leyhausen, Frank: Mitarbeiterbindung post Rente – Die übersehene Ressource. Bonn: managerSeminare, Heft 306, 2023. Online: https://www. managerseminare.de/ms_Artikel/Mitarbeiterbindung-post-Rente-Die- uebersehene-Ressource,283774

53. Anti-aging - Statistics & Facts: https://www.statista.com/topics/10423/anti- aging/#TopicOverview

54. Sontag, Susan: "The double standard of aging." London: *Saturday Review*, 23 September 1972

55. It's a study very much inspired by Hal Hershfield, Hershfield, Hal E., G. Elliott Wimmer, and Brian Knutson. "Saving for the future self: Neural measures of future self-continuity predict temporal discounting." Journal of Neuroscience 31, no. 12 (2011): 4288-4294.

56. Currently unpublished research conducted as part of a Knowledge Transfer Partnership between the University of Edinburgh and Aegon UK.

57. Buss, David M.: "Sex differences in human mate preferences: Evolutionary hypotheses tested in 37 cultures." *Behavioral and Brain Sciences*, 12(1), 1989, 1–14

58. Zuk, Marlene; Simmons, Leigh W.: "Sexual selection – A very short introduction." *Oxford: Oxford University Press*, 2018

59. Shields, Ali; Nock, Michael R; Ly Sophia; Manjaly, Priya; Mostaghimi, Arash; Barbieri, John S. "Evaluation of stigma toward individuals with acne." *JAMA Dermatology*. 2024;160(1):93–98

60. Sokolovsky, Jay: *The Cultural Context of Aging: Worldwide Perspectives*. London: Bloomsbury, 2008

61. Lock, Margaret: *Encounters with Aging: Mythologies of Menopause in Japan and North America*. Berkeley: University of California Press, 1993

62. Karpf, Anne: *How to Age*. London: The School of Life, 2014

63. "Wie wird man 100 Jahre alt? Altersforscher Helmut Luft gibt Rat." Frankfurt: *Frankfurter Allgemeine Zeitung*, 11 November 2024. https://www.faz.net/ aktuell/rhein-main/region-und-hessen/altersforschung-und-erfahrung-so-wird-man-hundert-jahre-110114324.html

64. Kinder, George: *The Seven Stages of Money Maturity: Understanding the Spirit and Value of Money in Your Life*. New York: Random House, 1999

65. Burnett, Dean: *Happy Brain: Where Happiness Comes From, and Why*. Guardian Faber: London, 2018

66. Aristotle: *The Nicomachean Ethics*. Oxford: Oxford University Press, 2016

67. De Botton, Alain: *The School of Life – an Emotional Education*. London: Penguin, 2019

68. Dolan, Paul: *Happiness by design. Finding pleasure and purpose in everyday life*. London: Penguin, 2014.

69. Dolan, Paul: *Happiness by design. Finding pleasure and purpose in everyday life*. London: Penguin, 2014

70. Benz, Christine: *How to Retire. 20 Lessons for a Happy, Successful, and Wealthy Retirement*. Harriman House, Petersfield, UK, p298

71. That said, here's an argument in favour of deferred gratification: remember that Dolan defines happiness as experiences of pleasure and purpose *over time*. Now, if you're feeling good about life being simpler and more enjoyable "one day" then that in itself can be an experience of pleasure over time. Don't beat yourself up for not living in the present enough if you're getting that experience of pleasure out of being a deferred gratification type of person.

72. Deci, Edward L.; Ryan, Richard M.: "The 'what' and 'why' of goal pursuits: Human needs and the self-determination of behavior." Psychological Inquiry, 11(4), 2000, 227–268

73. Kwon, Oh-Hyun.; Hong, Inho; Yang, Jung; Wohn, Donghee Y.; Meeyoung, Cha: "Urban green space and happiness in developed countries." *EPJ Data Science*. 10, 28 (2021). Astell-Burt, Thomas, Hartig, Terry; Eckermann, Simon; Nieuwenhuisen, Mark; McMunn, Anne; Frumkin, Howard; Feng; Xiaoqi, Feng: "More green, less lonely? A longitudinal cohort study." *International Epidemiological Association*, 2021, 1–12

74. By the way, we home-swap with other families. It's a great way to discover other lifestyles in other countries and saving a lot of money, too.

75. https://learningandwork.org.uk/resources/research-and-reports/adult-participation-in-learning-survey-2023/

76. Portnoy, Brian: *The Geometry of Wealth: How to Shape a Life of Money and Meaning*. Petersfield: Harriman House, 2018. p. 143

77. Lewis, Paul: "Our minds can be hijacked': the tech insiders who fear a smartphone dystopia." London: The Guardian, 2017. Online: https://urldefense.com/v3/__https://www.theguardian.com/technology/2017/oct/05/smartphone-addiction-silicon-valley-dystopia__;!!LTKUihUYLQ!lmbe4jKOZmdeKAlt6WeD8TV3_UAAAqKcqdRN8trvlO6dPwgoe-PDzYPsYxFZ_9WruhlYng9G5XtPvw7Ea2DPnGD_$))

78. Ramadan, Zahy: "Fooled in the relationship: How Amazon Prime members' sense of self-control counter-intuitively reinforces impulsive buying behavior." *Journal of Consumer Behavior*. Volume20, Issue6, November/December 2021, S. 1497–1507

79. European Commission: "Behavioural study on unfair commercial practices in the digital environment. Dark patterns and manipulative personalization: final report." Brussels, 2022. Online: https://urldefense.com/v3/__https://op.europa.eu/en/publication-detail/-/publication/606365bc-d58b-11ec-a95f-01aa75ed71a1/language-en__;!!LTKUihUYLQ!lmbe4jKOZmdeKAlt6WeD8TV3_UAAAqKcqdRN8trvlO6dPwgoe-PDzYPsYxFZ_9WruhlYng9G5XtPvw7Eay_rQQnD$

80. In an A/B test, various assumptions are tested in parallel – the successful one is implemented. The assumptions being tested often stem from psychological, behavioural science or evolutionary psychology insights. For instance, travel providers know, based on A/B tests, that a flight or accommodation is more likely to be booked if it's suggested that many other holidaymakers are also on the verge of booking the same trip.

81. Housel, Morgan: *The Psychology of Money: Timeless Lessons on Wealth, Greed, and Happiness.* Petersfield: Harriman House, 2020, p7

82. On a lighter note, I love this parody from "Charlie Brooker's Weekly Wipe" from 2015. It's a bit older, on the one hand, but yet still very contemporary in the way it depicts how the news only seemingly informs and educates but how they, rather, just leave you with a bad feeling in the end. Check it out for a good laugh. https://www.youtube.com/watch?v=HN2iVe8_Ato

83. Skowronek, Jeanette; Seifert, Andreas; Lindberg, Sven: "The mere presence of a smartphone reduces basal attentional performance." *Scientific Reports 13*, 2023

84. Eyal, Nir: Hooked: Wie Sie Produkte erschaffen, die süchtig machen. München: Redline Verlag, 2014

85. Lahitou, Jessicah: "Silicon Valley parents choose low & no tech schools. What about your kid's school?" Pasadena: The Good Men Project, 2018. Online: https://urldefense.com/v3/__https://goodmenproject.com/uncategorized/silicon-valley-parents-choose-low-no-tech-schools-thats-probably-not-the-tech-policy-at-your-kids-school/__;!!LTKUihUYLQ!lmbe4jKOZmdeKAlt6We D8TV3_UAAAqKcqdRN8trvlO6dPwgoe-PDzYPsYxFZ_9WruhlYng9G5XtPvw 7EawX_2s_m$

86. Hersch, Fred: *Good Things Happen Slowly – A Life in and Out of Jazz.* New York City: Crowne Archetype, 2017. 71

87. Hersch, Fred: *Good Things Happen Slowly – A Life in and Out of Jazz.* New York City: Crowne Archetype, 2017. 71

88. Hersch, Fred: *Good Things Happen Slowly – A Life in and Out of Jazz.* New York City: Crowne Archetype, 2017. 102

89. Hershfield, Hal E.: Goldstein, Daniel G.: Sharpe, William F.: Fox; Jesse, Yeykelvis, Leo; Carstensen, Laura L.; Bailenson, Jeremy: "Increasing saving behavior through age-progressed renderings of the future self." Chicago: *Journal of Marketing Research*, 48, 2009

90. Ashraf, Nava; Gharad, Bryan; Delfino, Alexia; Holmes, Emily, Iacovone, Leonardo; People, Ashley: "Learning to see the world's opportunities: The impact of imagery on entrepreneurial success." Working Paper, 2022. Online: https://poverty-action.org/sites/default/files/2023-07/learning-to-see-a-world-of-opportunities-working-paper-1.pdf__;!!LTKUihUYLQ!Imbe4jKOZmdeKAlt6WeD8TV3_UAAAqKcqdRN8trvlO6dPwgoe-PDzYPsYxFZ_9WruhlYng9G5XtPvw7Ea6OvyqQ9$

91. Ashraf, Nava; Gharad, Bryan; Delfino, Alexia; Holmes, Emily, Iacovone, Leonardo; People, Ashley: "Learning to see the world's opportunities: The impact of imagery on entrepreneurial success." Working Paper, 2022. Online: https://poverty-action.org/sites/default/files/2023-07/learning-to-see-a-world-of-opportunities-working-paper-1.pdf__;!!LTKUihUYLQ!Imbe4jKOZmdeKAlt6WeD8TV3_UAAAqKcqdRN8trvlO6dPwgoe-PDzYPsYxFZ_9WruhlYng9G5XtPvw7Ea6OvyqQ9$, p18

92. Hershfield, Hal: *Your Future Self. How to Make Tomorrow Better Today.* London: Piatkus, 2023

93. Covey, Stephen R.: *The 7 Habits of Highly Effective People.* London: Simon & Schuster, 1989

94. Ersner-Hershfield, Hal; Wimmer, Elliott G; Knutson, Brian: "Saving for the future self: Neural measures of future self-continuity predict temporal discounting." Oxford: *Social Cognitive and Affective Neuroscience*, Volume 4, Ausgabe 1, 2009

95. On this webpage, you can write a letter to your future self. You can also determine a point in the future when the letter is sent back to you. It's a lovely application of the insight: https://www.futureme.org/

96. Portnoy, Brian: The Geometry of Wealth, p96

97. Kudos to Meghaan Lurtz who expressed and explained this idea in Brendan Frazier's *Human Side of Money* podcast, episode from 11 October 2023 (A Blueprint for Conducting "Re-Discovery" Meetings With Long-Time Clients)

98. Rosenthal, Dorren; Moore, Susan (2018): "The psychology of retirement." https://www.bps.org.uk/psychologist/retirement-health-and-wellbeing

ACKNOWLEDGEMENTS

Where do I even begin with the thank yous? (A rhetorical question, of course, but it's a truism that behind the name on the cover page, there's a large number of people who made it happen.)

Starting with my work context: I'm immensely grateful for the fantastic support I've received at Aegon UK. First and foremost, there's Andy Manson – Aegon's Chief Marketing Officer – who embraced financial wellbeing in the 100-year life as an idea early on. He saw the unique space it occupies, the necessity of claiming that space and the importance of filling it with meaning. What we've built at Aegon was initially a bit 'out there' – a perspective that challenged conventional wisdom – but thanks to his vision and backing, it has become a well-established approach that's shaping the conversation.

Then there's Iain O'Connor, who has been an invaluable mentor – always generous with his time and advice, and particularly skilled at pushing me to spot opportunities, both within Aegon and beyond. His ability to challenge and guide in equal measure is something I've come to appreciate deeply. Our team leaders Laura Shanks and, earlier, Al Rhind, have also been steadfast supporters. Thank you all.

My research team – Tereza Anderson, Mauro Renna, Emily Shipp and Claire Shanks – has been instrumental not only in testing hypotheses on how to help people make better long-term decisions, but also in providing great lunchtime debates. Some were purely intellectual, others silly – both equally important in their own way.

More recently, I've had the pleasure of working with Kevin Carter and his team, Victoria Baird, Lauren Buchanan, Ellis Curtis, Emmie Harrison-West, Anna Neilson and many others in setting up our longevity education hub and the podcast. This is an exciting new chapter – one that I believe is essential in equipping people with the (self-) knowledge they need to navigate the realities of longer lives.

I've also learned an enormous amount from the many conversations I've had over the years. A particular thanks to Nava Ashraf, Neil Bage, Chris Budd, Daniel Crosby, Paul Dolan, Uland Grawe, Tina Harrison, Heiko Hauser, Sarah Newcomb, Brian Portnoy, Karl-Matthäus Schmidt and many others. And, of course, to those whose work I've benefited from but haven't had the chance to meet in person, notably Lynda Gratton and Andrew Scott.

A special thank you to those who read early drafts and provided invaluable feedback: Steven Cameron, Liz Green, Andy Manson (again), Mike Mansfield, Jonathan Sepulchre, Sophie van Dijk, Cameron Waldron and Monika Schneider

I'm grateful to the publishers, both the team at GABAL in Frankfurt (notably André Jünger and Nadine Fessler), where the German edition of this book appeared in October 2024, and the excellent team at LID Publishing (Alec Egan and Marin Liu, as well as Aiyana Curtis, Caroline Li and Teya Ucherdzhieva). Thanks also to Chris Budd for facilitating the connection.

When writing this book, I came to realize that I am, at heart, a social anthropologist. The finding that we're not stupid or irrational for finding navigating longevity hard; rather, we're just faced with a unique challenge in the history of humankind, was an epiphany moment for me. As an anthropologist, I was heavily influenced by two of my supervisors I had the privilege to work closely together with in my Berlin years – Jörg Niewöhner, now in Munich, and Stefan Beck, who, sadly, passed away far too young.

Then there's family. I recognize that my perspective has been shaped by a certain degree of privilege: I grew up in a stable home with access to opportunities that made my path smoother than it might have been otherwise. But I also know that this foundation wasn't accidental – it was the result of a lot of work. My parents put in the effort to balance work, health, financial security and family life, setting me on this path.

Closer to home, my deepest thanks go to my wife, Josi. She has kept me grounded in that all-important balance – work, health, family – and covered my back when writing took longer than planned. In this book I have, of course, argued that it's important to find *balanced* gratification, rather than just instant or delayed gratification.

In one of the footnotes though, I mention that we shouldn't beat ourselves up if we find ourselves thinking too much about our futures rather than fully appreciating the present. That was written with Josi and family in mind. Thinking about our future together – and the years ahead that, hopefully, we'll share – brings me as much joy and purpose as living in the moment.

ABOUT
THE AUTHOR

Thomas Mathar is an author, podcaster and speaker who helps shift the way we think about money. He joined Aegon UK in 2017 to lead the Centre for Behavioural Research, a team of psychologists and behavioural scientists dedicated to helping people make better long-term decisions about life and money. Working with financial advisers, employers and individuals, he brings fresh, practical insight to some of life's most challenging financial trade-offs.

More recently, Tom has taken on a leading role in Aegon's financial and longevity education efforts, where he focuses on helping people reframe their money mindset and make confident choices in an increasingly complex world. Whether in relation to planning for retirement, navigating a career transition or just trying to live well today without sacrificing tomorrow, Tom offers grounded, science-backed guidance to support a life of balance and purpose.

Tom holds a doctorate degree (hence his nickname Dr Tom) in social anthropology from Humboldt University in Berlin and later trained in behavioural economics at the London School of Economics. He is the author of *Financial Wellbeing* (in German) and has contributed to global policy discussions as a member of the World Economic Forum's 'Redesigning Retirement' working group. He is also an Associate at the University of Edinburgh Business School.

Originally from Hamburg, Tom now lives with his wife and children in the heart of Edinburgh, where he continues his mission to make money more human.